From Michaels grad Party,
She was a speaker!
Very good

Unfairly
Labeled

Unfairly Labeled

How Your Workplace Can Benefit From Ditching Generational Stereotypes

Jessica Kriegel

WILEY

This book is printed on acid-free paper. ∞

Copyright © 2016 by Jessica Kriegel. All rights reserved

Published by John Wiley & Sons, Inc., Hoboken, New Jersey
Published simultaneously in Canada

For general information about our other products and services, please contact our Customer Care Department within the United States at (800) 762-2974, outside the United States at (317) 572-3993 or fax (317) 572-4002.

Wiley publishes in a variety of print and electronic formats and by print-on-demand. Some material included with standard print versions of this book may not be included in e-books or in print-on-demand. If this book refers to media such as a CD or DVD that is not included in the version you purchased, you may download this material at http://booksupport.wiley.com. For more information about Wiley products, visit www.wiley.com.

Library of Congress Cataloging-in-Publication Data is available:
9781119220602 (hbk)
9781119220619 (ePDF)
9781119220626 (epub)

Cover image: ©iStock.com / 7io
Cover design: Wiley

Printed in the United States of America

10 9 8 7 6 5 4 3 2 1

For Mom

When I was five years old, I asked you what you wanted for your birthday. You said you wanted me to write you a book. Here it is. I couldn't have done it without you.

I love you.

Contents

Preface   *xi*
   Part One: The Problem with Labeling Generations   *xii*
   Part Two: Toolkit for Managers   *xiii*
   Part Three: Overcoming Generational Labels   *xiv*
Introduction: Taking Issue with Generational Issues   *xvii*
   Generation Exercise   *xviii*
   Perception Is Reality   *xx*
   How Labels Divide   *xxii*

I   THE PROBLEM WITH LABELING GENERATIONS   **1**

1   **Why We Stereotype**   **3**
   The Brain Makes Categories   6
   Predictions into Convictions   7
   The Ladder of Inference   9
   In-Group, Out-Group Dynamics   11

2   **Age versus Generation**   **15**
   Age Discrimination   17
   Age versus Generation   19
   Hiding Age Discrimination Behind Generation Labels   21
   Summary   24

3   **American Labels in a Global World**   **25**
   Generation Stereotypes in Other Cultures   27
   Summary   32

4   When Are the Labels Useful?   **35**
When a Label Is Useful: Marketing   38
The Better Way   40
Summary   43

II   TOOLKIT FOR MANAGERS   **45**

5   Employee Engagement   **47**
The Stereotype   49
Origins of the Stereotype   51
The Truth about Motivating Millennials   60
Overcoming the Stereotypes   63
Summary   71

6   Performance Management   **73**
The Stereotype   75
The Truth about Managing Millennial Performance   82
Overcoming the Stereotypes   86
Summary   93

7   Collaborative Teamwork   **95**
The Stereotype   97
The Error in Stereotypes   99
Overcoming the Stereotypes   102
Summary   107

8   Recruiting   **109**
The Stereotype   112
The Origin of the Stereotype   113
Overcoming the Stereotypes   116
Summary   120

9   Technology   **121**
The Stereotypes   123
The Origins of the Stereotype   124
Overcoming the Stereotypes   128
Summary   131

III OVERCOMING GENERATIONAL LABELS   **133**

10 Roadmap to Changing Your Organization's
  Culture   **135**
  Be a Maven   *137*
  Six Steps to Change   *138*
  Summary   *144*

11 Case Study 1   **145**
  Background   *147*
  The Request   *150*
  Needs Assessment   *152*
  Survey Results   *159*
  Results   *159*
  Focus Groups   *166*
  Training Programs   *168*
  Return on Investment Analysis   *185*
  Conclusion   *191*

12 Case Study 2   **193**
  Background   *195*
  The Request   *196*
  Needs Assessment: Survey   *198*
  Learning Style Differences by Generation *200*
  Learning Activity Preferences by Generation *200*
  Optimizing the Learning Environment   *207*
  Practical Implications   *209*

Resources: Case Study 2 Details   *211*
References   *217*
About the Author   *223*
Index   *225*

Preface

Generational labels do not work. When taken at face value, a generation is simply a description of a group of people born at about the same time, regarded collectively. The label itself is not bad. What is bad is the association our society has put on those labels. One cannot hear the word *millennial* without a swarm of preconceived notions filling the mind. The word has become sullied with ignorance. Although this is true for all generations, the situation is particularly egregious for the millennial generation (also known as generation Y). Most literature on generational issues focuses on this younger generation, particularly in the workplace. Although baby boomers, gen Xers, and the silent generation are not immune to stereotyping, they do not receive the same level of attention.

Assumptions about people cannot be made based on generational trends. The purpose of this book is to equip the professional workforce of America with the tools to overcome generational stereotypes and work better together.

It is a cycle that must be broken. I believe we would all benefit if we collectively took a reprieve from using generational labels. To relieve ourselves of unfair judgments and social baggage, I suggest we stop using generational labels until they've lost their charge.

This book is separated into three parts. The first part presents the existing problem with generational issues. The second part is a toolkit for managers. The third part provides a roadmap for overcoming generational stereotypes.

Part One: The Problem with Labeling Generations

We have become so enamored with the generational labels and the assumptions associated with them that our brains have used those definitions to construct social fictions. Managers, led astray by so called gen-experts, believe they understand the people on their team because they have read so much about "them"—the generation stereotype. Sometimes colleagues of different generations cannot get past the labels to a place of real understanding, and they often do not know they should try. Misunderstanding creates resentment; resentment creates difficulty communicating; miscommunication creates conflict. Part One of this book reviews in detail why generational labels do not work:

Chapter 1 reviews the history of generational labels and why we collectively have a tendency to stereotype, including the inherent brain processes that predispose us to the indiscriminate use of labels.

Chapter 2 takes a closer look at age versus generation discrimination. Age discrimination has long been illegal in the United States; generational discrimination is rampant. This chapter also includes an in-depth look at some of the published generational research that might mislead us into believing that false stereotypes are, in fact, true.

Chapter 3 analyzes the use of made-in-America labels in an increasingly global world. This adds another layer of complexity to generational misunderstanding and has consequences for global organizations. The United States is not alone in engaging in generational stereotyping. Many countries have their own labels, with different definitions and time-spans. Americans cannot assume that our cultural markers apply worldwide.

Chapter 4 asks whether generational labels are ever useful. The most common argument is that generational stereotypes are valid as a marketing tool when backed by extensive research. Marketers have a long history of segmenting the population into categories and creating marketing strategies to target them. Chapter 4 asks if this tactic really works, and, if so, might there be a better way?

Part Two: Toolkit for Managers

Managers have been getting advice since the sixth century BCE when the Chinese general Sun Tzu wrote *The Art of War*. In it, he recommends understanding the strengths and weaknesses of one's own organization, as well as those of the competition. Since then, management consulting has become one of the most lucrative global industries. In recent years, consultants have found gold in the field of generational studies. Unfortunately, these "experts" often lead managers astray. Their recommendations, intended to help foster understanding of generational differences, often lead to unfair discrimination with real economic and human consequences.

Part Two of this book is a toolkit for managers to help end the cycle of generational stereotyping. Each chapter reviews an area of management frequently thought to profit from generational segmentation, that is, recruitment, motivation of employees, performance management, and so forth.

Each chapter reviews:

- Existing stereotypes
- Advice frequently given to managers
- Misleading literature and studies on the topic
- Suggestions for change

Most of the focus in this section is placed on millennials. Millennials are not the only victims of stereotyping; however, they are, by far, the most targeted. There are fewer how-to articles or business consultants exaggerating the quirks of generation X and baby boomers. Though these chapters focus on millennials, it is important for the reader to remember that these lessons apply to all generations. The stereotyping and discrimination of millennials is a specific example that represents a much broader problem.

Chapter 5 on motivation begins Part Two. A host of assumptions are associated with motivating millennials, particularly pertaining to their outsized appetite for recognition, work/life balance, collaboration opportunities, career development, and compensation. This chapter will review the stereotypes and offer suggestions on how to motivate employees without resorting to one-size-fits-all definitions.

Chapter 6 addresses performance management: planning, reviewing, and developing employee performance.

Chapter 7 helps in creating a collaborative team.

Chapter 8 focuses on recruiting, specifically, how managers and organizations have been led astray in creating recruiting tactics to target specific generations.

Chapter 9 discusses technology. The toolkit would not be complete if it did not discuss the digital-native versus digital-immigrant myth so often discussed in the media.

Part Three: Overcoming Generational Labels

Whereas Part Two of this book offers advice at a microlevel to help leaders be more effective managers, Part Three offers macrolevel advice for leaders who want to improve their business culture by becoming aware of and eliminating generational labels. This section offers step-by-step advice on how to become agents for change, as well as two case studies that demonstrate how it has been done.

Chapter 10, the first chapter in Part Three, provides a roadmap for you to change your organization's culture. The six-step process will guide you to effecting change, even if you are not the CEO.

Chapter 11 is a case study that documents change in a global, high-tech organization. The Oracle Organization Development Consulting team identified intergenerational conflict occurring in their College Hire program and developed a training program that eased tensions. This case study looks at the business need for training and the sessions facilitated. A detailed return on investment (ROI) analysis documents a 700 percent increase in return on investment for the program developed.

Chapter 12 is a case study made of a railroad organization that was anticipating significant budgetary expenditures for employee training and technology upgrades. Frustrating media reports offering contradictory advice on the learning preferences of the different generations led a midlevel manager to question common research assumptions. He moved past the labels and helped focus the company. We will see how he did it and what benefits accrued.

My hope is that you will use this section of the book to envision real change within your organization and take your place in creating that change.

Introduction: Taking Issue with Generational Issues

Memorandum:
From: A woman in Human Resources at
a small nonprofit organization
To: Jessica Kriegel
Subject: Dealing with millennials

Jessica—I heard that you are studying generational issues. We are having an HR staff meeting in a couple weeks and were hoping you might join us. This organization is run by baby boomers who struggle to understand the new crop of millennial employees. We are experiencing a high attrition rate of those millennial employees as a result. Would you please come and speak to our group about how to deal with them effectively?

I understood her problem; this is a common concern in my field. I see many human resource (HR) professionals who are casting about in the sea of popular and scholarly literature looking for guidance on how to deal effectively with perceived generational differences. A few weeks later, I was in her conference room preparing for our workshop. A woman was setting up granola bars and fruit in the corner, while I looked for the projector cable. I was nervous—not so much about speaking in public but more about the reaction I anticipated from my controversial opening demonstration. Either I was going to make everything perfectly clear to them, or I was going to be asked to leave the premises. The woman who had emailed me walked in with a big smile and welcomed me with a handshake and a business card.

After introductions, I began the exercise that I hoped would clarify my subject. I asked the participants to form groups of three or four and instructed them to discuss and then write down a few words to describe each generation. For example, are millennials tech-savvy and traditionalists tech-averse? I gave them ten minutes.

But let's pause here. Before we go any further, join us in our virtual conference room and participate by completing the form.

Generation Exercise

Instructions: Spend 3–4 minutes writing down a few words that describe your perception of each generation:

Silent Generation (born before 1945):

Baby Boomers (born between 1945 and 1963):

Generation X (born between 1964 and 1979):

Millennials (born between 1980 and 2000):

As I walked around the room, I heard bits of each group's conversations.

"...nowadays, you can't get by with just a high school diploma..."

"...they have absolutely no common sense whatsoever..."

"...my father never would have done that..."

"...they're pretty family-oriented..."

" ... surprisingly antisocial, actually ... "

" ... you know, my daughter doesn't even use email ... "

" ... out-of-the-box thinkers ... "

" ... they lived through the Great Depression, which means they are really frugal ... "

" ... my three-year-old is already using an iPad. She knows how to open applications and play games. I didn't even show her how ... "

After 10 minutes, I brought their attention back to the front of the room and asked them to shout out their perceptions. As they did, I wrote their perceptions on a flipchart at the front of the room. The list ended up looking something like this:

Silent Generation (born before 1945):
work hard   stubborn   tech-averse   conservative
respect authority patriotic   traditional   prefer face to face

Baby Boomers (born between 1945 and 1963):
workaholic   loyal to employer   save the world   optimistic
prefer face   independent   money   family
  to face   motivated   oriented

Generation X (born between 1964 and 1979):
MTV generation latchkey kids   entrepreneurial prefer email
skeptical   cynical   fun   money driven

Millennials (born between 1980 and 2000):
collaborative   work/life balance text   tech-savvy   spoiled
need collabo-   save the world   entitled   need praise lazy
  ration

Perception Is Reality

When the list was complete, I posed two questions.

1. How many of you heard other people share a perception about a generation that you 100 percent agreed with?

    Most of the participants raised their hand.

2. How many of you heard other people share a perception about a generation that you 100 percent disagreed with?

    Most of the participants raised their hand.

Whatever their opinions, they were 100 percent convinced.

Then came the make-or-break moment when I would either win them over or be asked to leave:

"Now how would you feel if I did this?" I grabbed the big red flipchart marker and crossed off the word *millennial* and replaced it with the words *black people*.

An instant silence came over the room. The air was thickly uncomfortable, and I let the silence speak. After what felt like five minutes, but was surely less than 10 seconds, I finally asked, "Now that I have changed the labels, is it not immediately obvious how inappropriate this exercise has been? When I write *black people* at the top of the page and the adjectives below include words like *spoiled, lazy,* or *need praise*, it becomes instantly painful to read and ridiculous to contemplate. Yet we are perfectly comfortable labeling people of different ages. Why is that? Is it because when we talk about race we understand that we should not and must not classify millions of people with character traits—desirable or undesirable—based on only one common denominator? And yet when we talk about millennials or baby boomers or generation Xers, we do it all the time. How have we come to accept that everyone in this generation is the same? The only thing these 80 million people have in common is an age bracket that is 20 years long."

The first raised hand went up, and I braced for the worst. A woman, who looked to be in the baby boomer generation, stood and said: "I am so glad you said that. The exercise was really uncomfortable for me, and I couldn't pinpoint why. Now I get it. I've been to a lot of these generational talks, and this is the first time I've heard this side of the story. Usually, they talk about what makes us different."

Another hand went up. A man this time, who also looked to be a baby boomer, stood up. I could tell he was not on board yet. "You know, that may be true for most of these generalizations, but there are things you simply can't deny. For example, millennials are way more tech-savvy than traditionalists. They're into social media, and that's a fact."

I asked the man if he was on Facebook. He said he was, explaining: "I joined so I can look at pictures of my grandchildren." Then I asked him if he would be surprised to learn that I, a millennial (who works at a high-tech company, no less), have never had a Facebook account. Then I asked him if he had heard of the CEO of Oracle, Larry Ellison, a member of the silent generation who probably has a thing or two to say about being tech-savvy. He laughed and sat down.

Another man raised his hand and introduced himself as Sam. "I see your point," he said, "but there are some things I see in my own experience working with my millennial colleagues. There's a kid in my office who always has earbuds in. He has those earbuds in even when he walks to the Xerox machine. That is totally antisocial."

A millennial in the audience spoke up before I could respond. "You know, I have earbuds in all day long at my job, but 90 percent of the time there's nothing playing. I use my earbuds as my phone headset. I don't want to go through the hassle of pairing Bluetooth on and off for a regular headset, so it's just an easier way to be hands-free when I answer the phone. I don't even notice them anymore. It never occurred to me that it might seem antisocial to some people."

A second millennial in the audience chimed in, "I have ear-buds in all the time too, but I am listening to music. I need music. I grew up in the projects in a really chaotic home, and the only way for me to focus is if I can listen to music while I work. I'm just trying to do my best."

It was a powerful moment for me to watch Sam learn of two possible reasons why his millennial colleague might have earbuds in all day. It might have nothing to do with being antisocial.

Sam had heard somewhere in our pseudo-scientific, inter-generational pop culture that millennials are antisocial. Then he saw a millennial wearing earbuds and assumed it was because he did not want to socialize at work. It is possible that was the case, but there are also ten other possibilities Sam had not considered.

How Labels Divide

The labels that we assign to each generation create lines of separation almost arbitrarily drawn every 20 or so years. What makes 1980–2000 the defining millennial years, apart from the conveniently round numbers? And why do millennials have a 20-year-span, baby boomers a 19-year span, and Generation X a 16-year span? Most 16-year-olds are not having children. Sixteen years does not a generation make.

I know the year delineations are largely arbitrary, and yet I often find myself falling into the trap of identifying with my own stereotype.

For example, when I begin a presentation, I always list my accomplishments. I start by saying I work in organization development at Oracle, I have an MBA, and I wrote my doctoral dissertation on generational issues. I might name some awards I have won, or mention high-profile projects I've worked on. It can be a bit overboard. Why do I feel the need to justify my place at the front of the room? I have been invited. I belong there. My accomplishments are public record and have probably been previously discussed. Do I really need to reiterate? Is it because I'm a millennial? I know what preconceived notions I face before I open my mouth: I'm young. I was the youngest person in my MBA program, the youngest person in my doctoral program, and the youngest person on my team in my first job. As I result, I have always struggled with feeling judged, and I attribute this to ageist profiling. I've also felt as though I had to prove myself, which meant that I spent a lot of time early in my career either showing off or being defensive—which created a whole other set of problems. The label of *millennial* gave me an identity that I felt I had to battle, which resulted in me acting a certain way, which, in turn, reinforced people's perceptions of me as a "typical millennial." It was a negative and damaging self-fulfilling prophecy.

Ask the Gen-Experts

In recent years, an entire cottage industry of experts has arisen looking to throw light on these issues, but the results are vague and the research contradictory. Generation profiling is rampant in business and the media. "Experts" in generational issues, whom I like to call gen-experts, are writing books and articles, creating institutes and selling seminar tickets. In effect, they are selling their opinions to consumers hoping to find answers to complex questions—questions that seem new but have long been with us. Authors cannot even agree on which names to apply to the various generations. Millennials are sometimes called generation Y; traditionalists are also the silent generation; and generation X are often called baby busters. The catchy names are misleading, but they sell books.

Not only does each generation have several labels, but there are a couple of generations that share labels. Some authors call baby boomers "GenerationMe," but others apply that same name to millennials. According to the gen-experts, there are two entire generations, amounting to 156 million people, that tend toward the egocentric by prioritizing "Me"'. In their book, *Managing the Millennials*, Chip Espinoza, Mick Ukleja, and Craig Rusch (2010) called generation X the MTV generation; but Lynne Lancaster (2004) also used the term "MTV Generation" to label millennials. And what is an MTV generation anyway? Does watching MTV really define anyone?

Along with the confusion created by label making and name calling, the defining characteristics of each generation also change from author to author. For example, Neil Howe, one of the founders of generational studies, argues that millennials yearn for job security and want opportunities to advance within a single organization. However, in *Keeping the Millennials*, Joanne Sujansky and Jan Ferri-Reed warn that companies must cater to millennials or face high levels of turnover. Which one is it? Which option better fits an entire generation of 76 million people?

Other titles on the subject range from the positive (*Millennials Rising: The Next Great Generation*, by Neil Howe and William Strauss) to the not-so-positive (*Not Everyone Gets a Trophy: How to Manage Generation Y*, by Bruce Tulgan). Depending on the author, different perspectives with different labels define any one generation.

Few authors provide any quantitative research to support their claims on generational differences. Most of their research is done through case studies, interviews, and observation. For example, Howe and Strauss claim that generation X is the "latchkey kid" generation. They argue that having experienced high rates of parental divorce, they are a more cynical and depressed generation. That may strike a guilty chord in some baby boomers' hearts, but are there any data to support the claim?

Further, the president of the Generational-Targeted Marketing Corporation says generation X is the generation of "out-of-the-box thinkers," whereas Espinoza, Ukleja, and Rusch state that millennials are the ones who think out of the box. Does that mean that baby boomers do their thinking *inside* the box? Here we have a useless metaphor when two entire generations of Americans, amounting to 156 million people (or about half of the United States population), are described as thinking out of the box.

One of the most striking contradictions among the gen-experts deals with defining the generation that volunteers the most. Howe and Strauss called millennials the "volunteer generation," but Johnson and Johnson assign that label to baby boomers. The Bureau of Labor Statistics disagrees with both of them. Apparently, people aged 35–44 years old are most likely to volunteer (29.8 percent). That is generation X.

With so many gen-experts putting people into carelessly labeled, mythical boxes, how one perceives millennials or any labeled generation is influenced by the latest book read.

The Need for Information

We are acutely aware that society is changing due primarily to the seismic impact of technology in our lives, and we need to understand our changing world. Most of us have the best of intentions when we try to understand our colleagues who, for whatever reason, are different from us. Hence, the plethora of books, articles, and seminars on generational issues that are hungrily consumed by a confused populace. The gen-experts say that the multigenerational workforce is creating new dynamics to which we must adjust. However, these attitudes toward different generations are neither unique nor new. Long before the Internet, humans struggled to relate to one another across age lines. Texts from more than 2,000 years ago describe these same challenges:

> Children ... no longer rose from their seats when an elder entered the room; they contradicted their parents, chattered before company, gobbled up the dainties at table, and committed various offences against Hellenic tastes, such as crossing their legs. ... The counts of the indictment are luxury, bad manners, contempt for authority, disrespect to elders, and a love for chatter in place of exercise.
>
> **Kenneth John Freeman, quoting ancient texts,**
> **Dissertation published in 1907**
> **(commonly misattributed to Socrates)**

In this information age, when everyone can have a blog or a podcast, a veritable cottage industry has arisen to help us cope with the differences we experience among generations. Armed with good intentions, we define each other in order to understand each other. However, in so doing we oversimplify the complexity of human behavior. We are more comfortable defining the world around us in black-and-white terms rather than living in the discomfort of gray.

In this book, I hope to help you find comfort in the gray. Many millennials are lazy. Many others are not. Many others are sometimes lazy and sometimes not, and many others are lazy about certain things and not lazy about other things. The same can be said for any stereotype applied to any generation. You will not find easy answers in this book but, rather, tools to understand the deeply complex people in your life, regardless of the 20-year-long—generally accepted but largely arbitrary—age bracket they happen to fall within.

The Problem with Labeling Generations

1

Why We Stereotype

The first study of generational issues was published in 1953, before any generational labels had been coined. Baby boomers were not even baby boomers at that time. The term *baby boom* existed to signify instances of peak birth rates, but it did not refer to a generation or group of people. *The Coshocton Tribune* wrote about a baby boom in post-World War I England in 1920, for example. In December 1941, *The Galveston Daily News* reported that a baby boom had increased the population of the United States. The term *baby boomer* referring to those born after World War II in America was first used by Landon Jones in his 1980 book titled *Great Expectations: America and the Baby Boom Generation*.

Therefore, in 1953, when Roger Angell published in *Holiday* magazine the first study of a generation, titled *Youth and the World: USA*, still no label had been applied for the young adults they studied: individuals turning 21 in 1953. We now call them the silent generation. The author studied 23 young people from around the world and found that they had very few commonalities. They found no clear pattern or single voice that represented this group. Lacking any clear conclusion or definition, one of the photographers on the story, Robert Capa, called them "The generation X." (Ulrich & Harris, 2003) And so the first label was born—a label that indicated that no label was justified.

The term was then commandeered by Charles Hamblett and Jane Deverson (1964) to describe a completely different group. Their book, titled *Generation X*, described 1965-era teenagers, who are today's baby boomers. In the mid-1970s rock star Billy Idol popularized generation X by using the name for his band. Finally in 1991, Douglas Coupland wrote *Generation X: Tales for an Accelerated Culture*, referring to those reaching adulthood in the late-1980s, now still called generation X. For those keeping track at home, the label generation X has been used throughout the twentieth century to label three different generations and a rock band, despite the fact that it was originally coined to honor the diversity found in one generation.

Millennials (also known as generation Y) was the name coined in 1991 by Neil Howe and William Strauss in their book *Generations*. Then, the name-coining and generation-stereotyping began in earnest. As generational studies became popular in the media and as consultants saw opportunity knocking, further studies were commissioned and reported. Business leaders and human-resource managers saw this practice as a convenient shortcut on the road to understanding, motivating, and retaining their employees.

Despite the popularity of generational labeling, most people with whom I speak tend to agree when I suggest that generational definitions are overly simplistic stereotypes; yet our culture continues to use these reductive labels. If the perfectly normal human tendency to categorize and label were under our conscious control, the problem of stereotyping would be a smaller one. But it is not. Let's briefly examine our brain's role in our proclivity to rely on categories—even false and damaging ones that we consciously admit are unfair.

The Brain Makes Categories

Dr. David Rock (2009), the director of the Neuroleadership Institute and co-editor of the *Neuroleadership Journal*, coined the term *neuroleadership* to explain how the largely unconscious part of our brain handles change, as well as team collaboration and leadership style. One aspect of Rock's research explains how the brain craves certainty and avoids uncertainty when at all possible. Data gathered through measures of brain activity and hormonal secretions suggest that the brain sees uncertainty as a threat. The threat triggers an alert response in the limbic system.

The more ambiguity in any decision-making process, the greater the threat response in the brain. On the other hand, the lower the ambiguity level, the greater the sensation of reward.

As a result, we are constantly on the lookout, consciously and unconsciously, for ways to create certainty in an uncertain world; and in today's rapidly changing society, we look for all the comfortable predictability we can find.

One way to do this is to categorize and label things around us. The labels we assign to each generation help alleviate this sense of unpredictability. They allow us to believe that we know the people in that generation at least well enough to understand and possibly predict their behavior. If managers with new millennial employees can find an article that suggests millennials have entitlement issues but still need a lot of feedback, they can feel more confident in their roles as managers. They feel, at least, that they know what to expect and that they may be, even if just a little, ahead of the game. The truth, however, is much more individual, complex, and rife with possibilities. Millennial behavior cannot be predicted, but the brain does not like that.

Predictions into Convictions

Some may argue that they, themselves, have seen differences in generations. Their personal experience is enough to confirm the traits we associate with each generation. Rock's neuroleadership theory also demonstrates how the brain converts predictions into convictions.

The brain gathers information, converts the information into patterns, and stores the patterns as memories. These memories then become the foundation of beliefs that guide predictions for the future. Predicting patterns is a pleasure trigger that leads us to search for more patterns and predictability. And this leads inevitably to a condition rampant in all cultures: MSU (Making Stuff Up). Here's how it works:

When a stranger walks into the room, we instantly form a judgment about him or her based on appearances. We look at the clothes he or she is wearing; the way he or she stands; his or her hair, gender, skin color; and, yes, even his or her age group. Based on the information we've gathered in the past through our education, upbringing, and experiences, we have found patterns that we converted into memories. Based on those memories, our brain goes into prediction mode. We make stuff up (MSU) about intelligence, integrity, kindness, and personality. Unfortunately, we often act on these predictions and do not take the time to get to know the person in front of us. Our pleasure center was triggered based on our prediction; therefore, we do not always question our assumptions, revise our first impressions, or remain open to the reality that actually exists before us. Who has not been the victim of false first impressions? Who has not been treated unfairly by a manager who simply was not aware of his brain's tendency to Make Stuff Up?

MSU also affects how we interact with colleagues. Here is an example:

Jon is the chief marketing officer of a small start-up firm. He has been working on the new marketing strategy for months and is finally presenting his work to the chief executive officer (CEO) and his leadership team. Mia, the chief operating officer (COO), is in the room, but she is not focused. In fact, she spends most of her time looking at her phone. Mia, however, is a trusted adviser to the CEO, and Jon assumes because of her lack of attention, that she does not like his presentation. He begins building a prediction. He wonders if she has a problem with him personally and if that is clouding her judgment about his marketing plan. Midpresentation, he begins to plot a way to undermine her opinions and/or prevent her from speaking to the CEO about her reservations. He has unconsciously switched his focus from presenting a good plan to defending himself from the COO's possible future attack. But this is all MSU! In reality, Mia's son was called into the principal's office, and she has been getting text updates from her husband. Had she been paying attention, she would have been positive about Jon's presentation.

MSU is also how generational labels are formed, solidified, and acted upon. In the quest to reduce uncertainty, we have created an entire culture around generations, a culture that promises to alleviate anxiety and offers a plan for action, but is wholly inaccurate.

The Ladder of Inference

The example of Jon and Mia demonstrates how people can be, and often are, misunderstood. But how does this explain the entire industry of intelligent, educated gen-experts who misunderstand and mislabel whole sections of our society, labels seemingly unquestioned by professional human resources specialists? In order to understand how our brain's innocent misunderstanding can grow into widespread discrimination based on erroneous labels, we turn now to the Ladder of Inference model. Described in Peter Senge's (2006) popular book *The Fifth Discipline: The Art and Practice of the Learning Organization*, the Ladder of Inference model demonstrates the thinking process as humans move from a simple, observable piece of data to a belief or conclusion, and, ultimately, to action.

To illustrate the model, meet Melvin, a baby boomer, human-resources professional who is convinced that millennials do not behave appropriately in the workplace. His company has hired 200 college graduates in the past few years. As he sees more and more millennials at the office, his experience reinforces his belief. Melvin begins at the bottom of the ladder in the world of fact and observable data and moves up each step of the ladder, until he reaches MSU.

He Observes Objectively

Melvin is aware of his surroundings. He sees and hears things as a video camera might. What he records is that there are more millennials in his workplace than there used to be.

He Selects Data

Melvin sees hundreds of millennials every day. One day he enters the elevator and notices a woman in her 20s wearing a very short skirt and leopard-print high heels. This is the piece of data on which he begins to build his story.

He Adds Meaning

Melvin now applies his own values, culture, or experiences to the selected data. He believes that short skirts paired with leopard print high heels are inappropriate workplace attire.

He Makes an Assumption

Since Melvin believes the woman is wearing inappropriate workplace attire, he assumes that this woman shows poor judgment. He has also seen a male millennial wear sweatpants in the office and begins to recognize a theme around millennials and inappropriate clothing. This theme becomes a pattern—a brain-friendly, recurring pattern that attracts his attention.

He Draws Conclusions

He has now noticed multiple millennials wearing inappropriate attire in the workplace, and he draws the conclusion that millennials do not dress appropriately.

He Adopts Beliefs

Melvin adopts the belief that millennials are ignorant of social cues and workplace etiquette.

He Takes Action

Melvin then speaks with his friends and colleagues about how millennials are out of place, inappropriate, and unconcerned with workplace norms.

The Ladder of Inference model also demonstrates how the beliefs we adopt affect the data we select to focus on in the future. The next month, when Melvin sees another young person wearing what he feels is inappropriate attire, he walks through the same process. Because Melvin has a belief that millennials are ignorant of workplace etiquette, he pays no attention to the hundreds of millennials he sees every day who *do* dress appropriately. Melvin is now stuck in a reflexive loop.

The process of climbing up the Ladder of Inference explains our brain's tendency to create false judgment and also explains why generational stereotyping is so widely accepted in today's business culture. However, if generational stereotypes are wrong, why do many people identify with their own generational identities? Many people are proud to be associated with their generational label and the stereotypes that go with it. That, as we see below, is a by-product of social identity.

In-Group, Out-Group Dynamics

In the 1970s, Henri Tajfel and John Turner wrote extensively about in-group, out-group dynamics to explain social identity. The theory describes the process by which we classify people as "us" or "them." Tajfel and Turner (1979) state that this process takes place in three steps: social categorization, social identification, and social comparison.

The first step is social categorization. We categorize things in order to understand them. Our ability to categorize the world around us is necessary to our survival. Categorization allows us to understand the world more simply and helps remove some of the ambiguity with which our brain is uncomfortable. The categories can be very specific, like a family or a team at work, but they can also be broader, such as a religion, social class, race, or generation. Social categorization is the first step on the path to creating stereotypes.

The second step is social identification. Once the categories are in place, we self-identify. For example, high school students may identify themselves as jocks, goths, theater geeks, or nerds. Associating with a group helps them define their identity by understanding and mimicking appropriate behavior within the group. A sense of self-understanding and pride comes with being affiliated with a group. For example, the term *nerd* was once derogatory, but as more people identified with the category, a sense of belonging and understanding emerged. Now a large subculture proudly claims to be nerds, even adopting iconic role models, such as Bill Gates.

The final step in the social-identity process is social comparison, the process of comparing our group (the in-group) to the others (the out-group). To build self-esteem, members of the in-group must see themselves as better than the out-group. This is how sports team rivalries are formed and perpetuated. Red Sox and Yankees fans both see themselves as better than the other for various invented reasons: they may be more loyal, more vociferous, more logical, more down-to-earth, and so forth. Not only do we increase the status of our group to enhance our own self-esteem, but we also deflate the status of the out-group to inflate our own self-esteem. People tend to believe that the best generation is whatever generation they belong to.

Further, according to Tajfel and Turner, the characteristics we acquire as a result of identifying with a group are not artificial; they are real characteristics, adopted and practiced so that they become vital to a person's identity. This is why millennials are proud to be called millennials, despite the negative connotations often associated with that generation. The sam applies to for gen Xers and baby boomers.

Tajfel and Turner's findings are more than mere social science conjecture. In fact, a study by Gary Lewis and Timothy Bates (2010) at the University of Edinburgh revealed an underlying biological mechanism that seems to sense such things as social, racial, generational cues that drive us to identify with those groups. There is a genetic mechanism that drives us to favor members of our in-group, just as Tajfel and Turner described more than 30 years ago.

In my work, dealing with generational dynamics, I often find that each generation tends to hold less favorable judgments about the others. When I ask baby boomers to describe millennials, I will often hear negative descriptors, such as: "antisocial," "no common sense," "entitled," "lazy," and "selfish." On the other hand, when I ask millennials to describe baby boomers, I hear equally negative generalizations such as: "out of touch," "workaholic," "stubborn," and "technophobic."

One fascinating study of a single midwestern company, by Lester, Standifer, Schultz, and Windsor (2012) of the University of Wisconsin, examined actual versus perceived generational differences within the workplace. The researchers found evidence that each generation held mistaken beliefs about the others, based on the stereotypes perpetuated in our culture. For example, millennials perceived baby boomers as valuing formal authority much more than the baby boomers in the study claimed they did. Likewise, baby boomers perceived generation

X as valuing technology and social media more than the gen
Xers in the study claimed for themselves.

Our society seems to have determined that each generation
is different; our brains have eagerly agreed; and the media have
perpetuated the myth. Powerful social, psychological, and biological forces motivate us to create groups, label them, and act
on them. Combatting the errors in judgment—judgments we are
programmed to commit—requires effort and education.

2

Age versus Generation

It is well established that stereotyping in general is inappropriate in corporate America. Though it is common to discriminate based on race, gender, religion, and nationality, it is generally, not socially acceptable to do so. The exception is in stereotyping generations. In order to combat such stereotypes, we need first to be clear about what is really meant. Generational labels are created by the media and assigned according to the unique cultural environment in which its members were reared. Life-changing events and trends—such as wars, economic downturns, divorce rates, birth control, and even music styles—are thought to have uniquely and permanently marked each generation's members, qualitatively separating them from other generations. It becomes acceptable for gen-experts to lump members of a generation together because, as they say, these cultural events are a powerful force in homogenizing a group. This is how the gen-experts justify their assumptions about personalities and making predictions about behavior.

Age, on the other hand, is a chronological marker, a number. Though one can legitimately make assumptions about members of a certain age, these assumptions are usually based on biology or "life stage." In our culture, age and life-stage descriptions carry much less baggage and are much less vulnerable to institutionalized stereotyping, perhaps because there are laws against it.

Age Discrimination

The first complaints of age discrimination, submitted to the Equal Employment Opportunity Commission, were filed by female flight attendants in the 1960s. Age discrimination continues today but is less overt. A study by Joanna Lahey (2005), published by the Boston College Center for Retirement Research, found that organizations were 40 percent more likely to ask a young person back for a second interview than job applicants over the age of 50.

Age discrimination is not limited to recruiting efforts, however. It is also a factor in promotions and internal advancement. A colleague once told me a story of her experience facilitating a talent development exercise at a major distribution company. As part of an organization-wide initiative, talent development specialists were assisting upper management in identifying employees with a high potential for advancement within the corporation. Once identified, the chosen employees would be rewarded with specialized perks, such as additional learning and development opportunities. They were, in effect, being put on a fast track to success. At one point, a group of senior leaders focused on an older gentleman in his late 50s. He fit all the criteria that define someone with high potential. He was performing at high levels, was committed to the organization, and aspired for a promotion within his team. However, the committee unanimously agreed that he was not a contender for advanced opportunity. How, they argued, could he possibly grow in the organization since he was so "long in the tooth."

This type of age discrimination is, of course, illegal. The Age Discrimination in Employment Act (ADEA) is a federal law enacted to protect job applicants and employees over the age of 39 from age-based discrimination in all aspects of employment. Enacted in 1967, its roots were in Title VII of the 1964 Civil Rights Act of 1964. Title VII prohibited discrimination in employment based on race, color, sex, national origin, or religion. Age was noticeably missing from Title VII, so three years later the ADEA was enacted by the U.S. Senate and the House of Representatives to include a provision addressing age.

There is also a provision addressing harassment. Harassment is illegal when it is so frequent or severe that it creates a hostile or offensive work environment. One could argue that the entire field of generational studies falls into this category. However the ADEA applies only to individuals over the age of 40. Therefore, using this logic, it would seem that the rampant negative stereotyping of millennials is legal, but when applied to baby boomers it is illegal!

Age versus Generation

The fact is that many of the characteristics and stereotypes we attribute to the generations are often life-stage issues that come and go as the person ages. Let's look at two examples of generational stereotypes, as defined by the gen-experts that upon further investigation are truly based on age (or life stage).

The silent generation, born before 1945, has been described as the frugal generation because the members (or their parents) of that generation (or their parents) lived through the Great Depression. This experience has supposedly shaped them to be cost-conscious. But, as anyone who has taken a basic logic or statistics course knows, correlation does not imply causation. If it is true that members of the silent generation are more frugal, it might be better explained by their life stage, rather than their generation.

The vast majority of the members of this generation are retired. The labor force participation rate for individuals over the age of 65 is 11.5 percent in the United States, as compared with 83.7 percent for individuals between the ages of 25 to 54 (Monthly Labor Review, 2013). Could it be that frugality is a natural consequence of living on a fixed income?

Taking it a step further, the post-World War II era was when Americans were said to be keeping up with the Joneses. Adults were using materialism to project success in their careers. In the 1950s, when this trend was taking shape, many in the silent generation were young adults. The silent generation was not frugal in the 50s, perhaps the silent generation's current frugal behaviors have nothing to do with the Great Depression after all.

Another example is generation X. This generation is often categorized as being more family-oriented. An article by Susan Thomas in the *Wall Street Journal* (2011) asserted that since generation X was the first generation to experience significant divorce rates, they would naturally be more focused on the family as a result of the trauma—a giant jump to a highly suspect conclusion. Let's look more closely at the data: The year the article was published, generation Xers were between the ages of 36 and 51. These are prime child-rearing years. Isn't it more likely that the orientation toward family that the newspaper associated with generation X was simply due to biological age or life stage, and not the trauma of divorce?

If a generation were truly to be defined by the historical and cultural circumstances in which its members were reared, then presumably members' defining traits would remain the same as they aged: once frugal, always frugal; once family oriented, always family oriented. However, this is not the case. In 2014, The Nielsen Company, a leading market research firm, polled millennials and baby boomers, asking what made their generation unique (*Millennials—Breaking the Myths*). Millennials ranked "technology use" first (24 percent), followed by "music/pop culture" (11 percent). Baby boomers, on the other hand, rated "work ethic" as the most defining characteristic of their generation. Do these characteristics define the generation or, rather, do they define stages of normal development and maturity? Think back to when the baby boomers were in their late teens and early 20s. These were the 1960s, when peace, love, and hippie culture emerged to a rock-and-roll soundtrack. Had Nielsen asked these same baby boomers the same question when they were younger, they might have answered "music" or "cultural revolution." They might even have stated "technology," referring, of course, to the technology that existed at the time: televisions, hi-fi sounds systems, and transistor radios. But would baby boomers in the 1960s have said "work ethic"?

Isn't it possible or, actually, likely that today's millennials, as they mature in the real world, will soon claim "work ethic" as a sought-after descriptor on their job applications? And, even later, might they not consider frugality as important to their success in later life?

Examples such as these are endless and yet the media and gen-experts still perpetuate the myth of generational differences. In fact, generational differences are the masks behind which age discrimination hides.

Hiding Age Discrimination Behind Generation Labels

It seems that the media find it perfectly appropriate to discuss issues of ageism, but only when it is disguised by the word *generation*. Today, a mountain of published works explains, analyzes, and describes the work habits, dress codes, moral codes, and ambitions (or lack thereof) of each generation.

The extent of the problem can be demonstrated by a search engine's list of articles on working with millennials. The search will pull up endless lists of tips:

- Five tips on how to manage millennials.
- Three reasons millennials are getting fired.
- Ten ways to engage your millennial employees.

These articles, often posted by web-content factories, are capitalizing on industry's need to bridge the talent gap, the employee vacuum caused by retiring baby boomers. Companies need to fill the gap with younger employees and keep them happy. They are, therefore, hungry for answers. The gen-experts provide answers in the form of quick tips, compiled with a minimum of research, on how to attract and work with those most likely to be entering the job market. But they also mislead readers into believing that the majority of millennials share certain traits and imply that other generations do not. Imagine if I were to swap out the word *millennial* for an actual age (in this case an older one).

- Five tips on how to manage your 60-year-olds.
- Three reasons why 60-year-olds are getting fired.
- Ten ways to engage your 60-year-old employees.

Suddenly the articles do not seem as harmless.

A conclusion that might be reached is that the gen-experts cannot be trusted. Most of the time their articles and books provide no research to support their hypotheses. Even when research is provided, however, it is often misleading and unreliable. For example, Jean Twenge and Stacey Campbell (2008) co-authored a meta-study in the *Journal of Managerial Psychology* titled "Generational Differences in Psychological Traits and Their Impact on the Workplace." Twenge, the primary author of the study and a well-known author, speaker, and consultant in generational studies, takes questionable liberties in representing her research. The article takes a longitudinal look at generational differences in a metastudy that reviews data from 1.4 million respondents over the course of 80 years. The data have been gathered from various research reports measuring personality, attitude, and behavior from college-age students. By comparing all 1.4 million individuals at approximately the same age over the course of multiple decades, the authors claim to separate generational effects from life stage. Though the data are valuable, it hardly justifies the exaggerated assumptions about the generations that the authors claim based on their findings.

Let's look at some of their findings, followed by some of Twenge and Campbell's conclusions.

The Need for Social Approval Has Decreased

Using Crowne and Marlowe's (1960) social desirability scale, the authors measured what they call "the need for social approval" of every generation. They described that the higher the score, the more concerned people are with the impression they make on others and the more likely they are to conform. The authors continue to infer that respondents are more likely to dress and act accordingly. However, the scale was not developed to determine conformity of dress. The scale measures the degree to which individuals inflate their strengths and achievements or deny their deficiencies when completing questionnaires that assess their personality: that is, the extent to which individuals attempt to depict themselves as similar to the norms and standards of their society. The results reveal that the silent generation scored highest on this scale; baby boomers scored a bit lower, and generation X and millennials scored equally at historically low levels.

Labeling this finding as "the need for social approval has decreased" is misleading. It is not the need to be approved by society that has decreased, but rather the need for the respondents to depict themselves as similar to the norms of society. The authors then describe how millennials rolled out of bed and into their college classes wearing wrinkled sweat pants and flip-flops and that they bring this informality of dress to the workplace as well. The research could imply that our culture has transitioned from all members needing to be the same as one another to no longer needing to be so. Does it not have as much to do with social acceptance and embracing diversity than it does with dressing appropriately in the workplace? And what part of the research justifies the authors' description of millennials rolling out of bed and into their college classes wearing wrinkled sweat pants and flip-flops?

Depression and Anxiety Have Increased

The authors state that of Americans born before 1915, only 1 to 2 percent reported experiencing a major depressive episode, whereas 21 percent of millennials reported experiencing a major depression by the time they turned 18. In addition, millennials were 71 percent more anxious than baby boomers and 85 percent more anxious than the silent generation. Although the data for this finding are compelling, the authors conclude that millennials become anxious when employers do not give them direction or clarity regarding their role. However, no data support this claim. Furthermore, the authors do not apply this same logic to older generations, who might also become stressed as a result of a lack of managerial direction.

Summary

Even the most academic studies, authored by the most respected experts in the field of generational differences, exaggerate content in a way that misleads the reader. We must begin to see the research for what it sometimes is: an opportunistic fad that exaggerates differences between generations in an overly simplistic fashion to no real benefit to understanding.

Returning to the original question: When is it an age issue and when is it a generational issue? The answer remains the same. We must avoid the natural human tendency to categorize, label, and stereotype individuals based on their age or generation. Instead, we must do the less sexy work of understanding the individuals in front of us, their motivations, tendencies, personality quirks, and preferences. Anything else in the workplace is simply discrimination.

3

American Labels in a Global World

Globalization of the workforce has transformed the modern-day labor pool. According to a 2014 White House report, managers in the United States are dealing with the most diverse group of employees in history. In 2014, Foreign-born employees made up 16.5 percent of the United States workforce in 2014. That represents a significant portion of our U.S.-based employees. In addition to these employees, there are the thousands of foreign-based employees who are associated with American companies through their global networks. Yet, despite this well-documented trend, generational labels are still part of our common business vocabulary, even though they are based on a middle-income, American archetype of a person born and reared in the United States.

Generation Stereotypes in Other Cultures

The American-born concept of generational stereotyping has been exported and adapted to other cultures. Hole, Le Zhong, and Schwartz (2010) chronicle cultural differences in generational labels in their report: *"Talking About Whose Generation"*? Generational differences, as we've seen, are supposedly shaped by significant historical and cultural events; it is obvious that "significant events" vary from culture to culture. For example, the kick-off year for baby boomers, 1945, may have had a major impact for North American, European, and Japanese workers, but not for the entire world.

Countries with Their Own Labels and Cultural Markers

China. China is an important example of how generational labels vary among countries; China has entirely different generational labels and defining years that pertain to its own historical shifts. The words *baby boomer, gen Xer*, and *millennial* are not a part of normal discourse in China. However, the country's citizens are not immune from generation identification and classification. China deals with their post-1950, post-1960, post-1970, post-1980, post-1990, and post-2000 "generations":

- The post-1950 generation came of age with the founding of the People's Republic in 1949.
- The post-1960 generation is marked by the Great Leap Forward of 1960, an economic and social campaign by the Communist Party of China that eventually led to the Great Chinese Famine.
- The post-1970 generation was the first generation significantly influenced by the West. Additionally, the members of the generation had more flexibility in choosing their own careers and some limited opportunities to work in multinational companies.
- The post-1980 generation was the first born after China's adoption of the One-Child Policy, a policy that radically changed the definition and structure of family.
- The post-1990 generation was the first born after the Tiananmen Square protests of 1989.
- The post-2000 generation is also sometimes referred to as generation Z and is defined by the adoption of digital technology and the Internet.

Using China as the example, we can more easily see the leaps of logic that lie at the root of generational stereotyping, as obvious questions arise:

How long is a generation? It has traditionally been 20 years, defined by the time it takes a child to reach maturity. But while the United States defines only three generations since 1945, China has six.

How can managers define their employees as stereotypical millennials with all the cultural associations that the label represents, if they were raised in China? Most managers in the United States are unaware of the Chinese generational labels and stereotypes that come with them.

What must it feel like for a foreign-born employee to listen to the gen-experts predict their behavior when they did not live through the U.S. cultural events that supposedly define them?

Japan. Japan provides another example, with its own set of generations and labels:

- The first baby boomers from 1946 to 1950.
- The danso generation from 1951 to 1960.
- The shinjinrui generation from 1961 to1970.
- The second baby-boomer generation from 1971 to 1975.
- The postbubble generation from 1976 to 1987.
- The shinjinrui junior generation from 1986 to 1995.
- The yutori generation from 1987 to 2012.

These generational definitions are equally as arbitrary as those in the United States. They range from being only 4 years long (first baby boomers) to 25 years long (the yutori).

South Africa.   South Africa has a unique set of labels and definitions that correspond to its significant historical events. The election of 1994 in South Africa marked the transition from the system of apartheid to majority rule. Members of the "Born Free" generation are those born in the years 1994 to the present.

South Korea. South Korea uses a remarkably complicated labeling system for its generations. South Koreans born from 1960 to 1969 are known as the 386 generation. The label, coined in the 1990s, was named after the Intel 80386 microprocessor, also known as the 386. It refers to people who were (then) in their 30s, who went to college in the 1980s, and were born in the 1960s. As time went on and the generation got older, they eventually became known as the 486 generation.

India. India has three generations, roughly correlated to the Western generations in defining years, but marked by different historical events:

- The partition generation, 1944–1963, is defined by India's independence from British rule.
- The transition generation, 1964–1983, has sympathy for the previous generation's struggles, but supposedly do not feel the struggle as deeply.
- The postliberalization generation, 1984–1993, enjoys India's economic liberalization, which began during their childhood.

Russia. Russia adds even further confusion to generational studies. Russia (along with other countries) uses the same labels as America but assigns opposite personality traits to those individuals. The defining cultural events and stereotypes associated with Russian generations are different but the labels remain the same:

- Western baby boomers grew up in a post-Depression, postwar, materialistic era, whereas Soviet baby boomers lived in a state-controlled economy. Therefore, Western baby boomers are considered individualistic, whereas Soviet baby boomers are known for their collectivism.

- Western gen Xers supposedly value work-life balance above all else, whereas Russian gen Xers, growing up in a time of hyperinflation after the fall of the Soviet Union, are thought to be obsessed with creating wealth.
- Russian millennials are known for being intensely nationalistic, whereas American millennials are sometimes described as the least patriotic generation.

So how should the Russian gen Xer who moves to the United States for college be described? Which traits would that gen Xer have?

Overcoming Western Dominance in a Global Environment

There are studies that examine generational differences through a global lens. A study by Universum described significant differences on a wide range of factors, including values, priorities, and motivation, when millennials are studied by region, adding evidence that diversity exists among members of generations in the world community.

Another global study, conducted by PricewaterhouseCoopers (PwC; 2013) in partnership with the London Business School and the University of Southern California, also examined generational issues in a global workforce. The study examined generational differences across 18 global territories, and included 44,000 anonymous survey respondents, 300 interviews, 30 focus groups, and an online jam session involving 1,000 employees. The results reveal that traits and needs of millennials are not universal, meaning that employees in different regions may require different managerial styles.

In reviewing any literature, however, I caution the reader to tread carefully. Although the PwC study was well done, the authors' analysis of the results were sometimes misleading. The authors found generational differences even where they did not exist. For example, the first listed finding of the study was that millennials value work/life balance; however, the second listed finding was that other generations value work/life balance just as much. Would it not be more accurate to report that work/life balance is highly valued by all generations and present it as one finding?

Meanwhile, the Universum study of more than 16,000 millennials in 43 countries found that millennials valued work/life balance, but it also found that different millennials defined work/life balance differently. Although work/life balance meant flexible working hours for some, it meant a convenient work location for others, and recognition from managers to others still. The diversity is vast.

Yet, there are still efforts to divide and categorize cross-global generations into American categories. Mark McCrindle (2013), self-described as an Australian futurist and social commentator on generational issues, published a chart of the five Global Generations defined by name, year of birth, and social influences. The social influences he cites in his study are almost entirely from the West and include musicians, United States presidents, and television shows produced in the United States. He makes no mention of the cultural or historical experiences outside the Western world.

Summary

As consumers and workers become more and more virtually connected, as more and more people immigrate and emigrate, as the world becomes more and more a melting pot, the generational stereotypes become even less relevant. Managers working in a global environment must be sensitive not only to the perils of generational stereotypes, but the added danger of applying American labels to a global workforce.

As would be expected, each of these generations, regardless of country or label, is associated with its own set of stereotypes and defining characteristics. The model of sorting the population into overly simplified "personality buckets" is a practice that is not unique to America but is exported from America to other countries as well.

4

When Are the Labels Useful?

have argued, thus far, that the generation labels, so easily bandied about in business literature, are largely inaccurate. I have examined commonly used stereotypes, paying particular attention to studies that use inconsistent data and authors who draw illogical conclusions, and I have demonstrated that gross generational stereotyping often leads to misunderstandings and unfair expectations. Poor management decisions based on stereotyping lead to unnecessary job loss, missed opportunities for current employees and job seekers, and inaccurate communication between employees.

I am not arguing, however, that generation labels should be discarded as completely useless. There are age-based, generational trends. Our culture is changing very rapidly. In many ways, people function differently now than they did even a generation ago. I do, emphatically, take issue, however, with how we use broad trends to narrowly label and define the individuals around us.

There is no substitute for personal understanding and communication. Let us imagine a manager who reads a report from the Pew Research Center, or more problematically, a media summary of the study. The data show that younger generations are more likely to believe that new technology makes life easier. Seventy-four percent of millennials think so; whereas 69 percent of gen Xers, 60 percent of baby boomers, and 50 percent of the silent generation agree. This is a trend: Younger generations are more likely to believe that life—and their jobs—will become easier with new technology. Only the silent generation is on the fence. A manager with an employee who is a member of that wavering silent generation has a 50/50 chance of guessing whether they believe new technology makes life easier. Furthermore, even on a team of four millennials, it is possible that at least one of them might feel that new technology, in fact, does not make life easier. Rather than making a decision based on a trend, the manager should communicate and engage with his or her team.

When a Label Is Useful: Marketing

Marketing is one area in which generational labels do make sense. Trends are crucial for marketers. It is their stock in trade; it is a science. Market researchers have a long history of segmenting the population into broad categories composed of individuals with common interests and priorities and then designing a marketing strategy to target them. New moms, New Yorkers, chief HR officers, and, yes, millennials are some examples of these market segments. Marketers know that they are making assumptions and generalizations about the people in these segments. They know they cannot be 100 percent accurate in their market assumptions. They are aiming for the trend and do not concern themselves with "outliers." Sales and marketing professionals today have enthusiastically grasped generational labels as a way to commodify their expertise.

Tips for Marketing to Millennials

Following is the advice most commonly given on how to market to millennials:

- Get digital.
- Be engaging.
- Be creative and adventurous.

These three suggestions stem from the view that millennials are digital natives, have shorter attention spans, are better connected, and are, well, young. Let us examine these recommendations one at a time.

Get Digital. Marketing professionals are frequently advising clients to get digital when trying to reach millennials. We are told print is dead for millennials. Young consumers use online tools, such as social media, Pandora, and YouTube. According to the Pew Research Center, 85 percent of millennials own a smartphone. To reach the millennial market, markets need to optimize their advertising for smartphones and tablets, place their content online in visible locations, and make the messages visually appealing and easily shared with others.

Be Engaging.   Given that millennials are digital natives, they are said to have a higher level of intimacy with technology than other generations. Millennials not only consume content, they also produce and interact with content. More than any other generation, millennials sleep with their cell phone on or right next to their bed (Pew Research Center). Because of this increasing dependency, successful campaigns will ask consumers to engage. Once engaged, they are identified and targeted.

As digital natives, millennials have long been content creators. It is not enough, supposedly, for them to consume content; they must be contributors. Growing up with Wikipedia, Instagram, Twitter, and YouTube, they have become accustomed to the interactive nature of Web 2.0. To truly grab their attention, marketers are advised to encourage millennials' participation in conversations, surveys, and contests. Ideally, they will be completely engaged when they post their own stories, pictures, or videos. It might be helpful to remember that Wikipedia was founded on, and continues to thrive on, the principles represented by their acronymic title: "What I Know Is," paired with the "pedia" from encyclopedia, the trustworthy fount of traditional knowledge.

Be Creative and Adventurous.   Being online all day means being bombarded with masses of inventive attention-stealers: intrusive ads, pop-ups, notifications, tweets, and flags. To attract millennials, marketers need to be heard above the disturbing noise and hit their target market with attention-grabbing content. That has been translated to suggest strategies, such as viral videos, funny campaigns, and other types of unusual creative content that will hopefully be shared. Safe marketing will not reach the millennial market. Brands need to be willing to take risks and invent remarkable content, that is, anything unexpected. This is not bad advice. The three points mentioned earlier for marketing to millennials—get digital, be engaging, and be creative—are strong tools for reaching an audience. Stereotyping may indeed, work in marketing, but there is a better way.

The Better Way

In late 2014, Sheryl Sandberg, Facebook's Chief Operating Officer (COO) and the author of *Lean In*, led an *Advertising Week* panel called *Rethinking Marketing to Women* (Fallon, 2014) The panel explored gender roles in global advertising campaigns, focusing specifically on how women are stereotyped. Andrew Robertson, the CEO of a global advertising agency, BBDO Worldwide, shared that there is an easy defense for using stereotypes in marketing: it works. But, he added, there is a better way. The following are three tips that explore the better way.

Generations Are Too Broad for Grouping Target Markets

During the days of *Mad Men*, when television and print were the primary advertising modalities, demographic groupings, such as "young mother" or "older male veteran," were useful tools for classifying broad audiences into narrower niches. Today, however, due to self-defining social networks and technological advances, a huge amount of behavioral data is available for making ever-more targeted campaigns to potential customers. This market fragmentation is becoming increasingly refined because we now have easily available, intimate details of consumers' lives, including their hobbies, friends, job interests, and vacation plans. This means that companies now have the ability to target consumers based on the much more specific and accurate information on individual behaviors, rather than on outdated and unsupported stereotypes.

Generations are too broad of a grouping to truly be effective. Although some millennials are still in high school, others are divorced parents. Although some millennials are waiters in the Midwest, others are CEOs in Silicon Valley. It is hard to think of any unifying cause or product that rallies an entire generation. Though broad generalizations about millennials may seem to be shortcuts for marketers, they are not efficient enough to be truly effective.

Instead, marketers can now segment any desirable group, using a variety of other qualifying demographics, such as education or income. A 2015 study, published by Futurecast, a market research firm, examined only affluent millennials. They defined affluent as those with an annual household income of over $100,000. This group makes up only 7 percent of the millennial population. They further segmented these affluent millennials into four target markets: big-city bachelors, forward-thinking families, calculated go-getters, and active influencers. This is an excellent example of targeting like-minded markets that are not overly broad and can be useful to marketers. Other suggestions include creating subtargets determined by media use, geographical location, or profession, to name just a few.

Marketing to the Generations Can Be Bad for Your Brand

Marketing to generational demographics can create some unintended and negative results. Whole Foods, for example, recently announced a new chain of stores that would be designed for the millennial generation. They described each new store as modern, with a streamlined design that would incorporate innovative technology and a curated selection of low-priced organic and natural food. Upon releasing their ads for the new stores, they were hit with a vociferous backlash for excluding nonmillennials. Whole Foods was accused of overtly implying that gen X and baby-boomer shoppers would be content to shop in more inefficient, more expensive, and poorly designed stores.

No matter the context, using generational labels is divisive. It perpetuates the illusion that "we" are different from "them." The labels, used in any context, create separateness and encourage the stereotyping associated with social identity. It also leads to feelings of being left out, which in turn alienates otherwise potential buyers.

Technology Use Leads to Changing Consumer Expectations for All Generations

Proponents of generational labels disagree with me and argue that it would be silly to turn a blind eye to the differences among the generations. Millennials, for example, have grown up using the technology that baby boomers did not have as children; their exposure at a young age to these tools has shaped their lives in ways to which baby boomers cannot relate. However, I am suggesting that this theory might unfairly condemn digital immigrants to a lifetime of being outsiders.

High-tech companies are often guilty of this generational alienation. Salesforce, one of the most highly valued cloud computing companies operating in customer relationship management (CRM), posted an article on their blog entitled "5 Ways Millennials Are Re-defining the Customer Experience" (Frumkin, 2015). The article asserts that, thanks to the speed of technology, millennials value their time highly and want fast response times. Do baby boomers or gen Xers love waiting around for customer service? It is not millennials that have changed consumer expectations, it is technology. And all technology users are affected, regardless of age.

Summary

Advertisers have used labels to describe potential market groups for decades. However, modern-day technology allows marketers to be more specific in their targeting practices. It also relieves them of using divisive generational labels that can be off-putting for those left out. These suggestions in marketing, incidentally, are also the main arguments of this book. Whereas a marketer will waste money if the target market is too broad, managers who makes broad assumptions will suffer communication break-downs with the employees. Generational labels in the workplace foster an "us versus them" culture that hinders collaboration and cooperation.

Because generational labels have become so deeply associated with often unfair stereotypes, we need to correct our course. A collective commitment to avoiding generational labels may remove stigma, associated with each generation. This is particularly true in the workplace, where colleagues, managers, and employees need to understand one another beyond the stereotype. The following section is a toolkit for corporate professionals to identify the stereotypes and overcome them.

Toolkit for Managers

5

Employee Engagement

There are seven factors to employee engagement often discussed in generational literature: recognition and praise, meaningful work, making a positive impact in the world, work/life balance, a collaborative work environment, opportunities for advancement, and compensation. The gen-experts commonly cite these factors as necessary to keeping millennials happy. The chapter will examine the origins of these stereotypes and what advice commonly follows. Finally, we will look at how to identify stereotypes, break them, and move toward best practices in engaging employees, regardless of age.

The Stereotype

Meet Ryan, the typical millennial as described in gen-expert literature. Ryan is a fresh-out-of-college new hire. He is a hard-to-please employee with high expectations. He is confident in his technical skills but limited in work experience. His manager works hard to meet his sometimes unrealistic demands or risks losing him to the competition.

The Precedine is a gen-experts's caricature of the typical millennial. Although some recognize the myth behind this caricature, such stereotypes continue to confuse.

Justification for the Stereotype

Where do the negative assumptions and steroetypes come from? Let us look at the supposed rationale.

Millennials Are in Need of Constant Praise and Encouragement. Because they grew up in the age of participation trophies, millennials are accustomed to being praised, even when they do not perform at a high standard. They are spoiled and unrealistic but will leave the company if their egos are not fed praise on a regular basis.

Millennials Need to Be Engaged in "Meaningful" Work.

Not only do millennials need to know they are doing a good job, they need to know they are doing an *important* job. They are motivated by progress and creativity. They must be doing meaningful work because, unlike their older colleagues, they are not happy simply to punch a timecard in and out.

Millennials Are Our Most Socially Conscious Generation.

Millennials' desire for giving back also applies to their company as well. They are a socially conscious generation who intend to make a difference. They also desire time off from work to volunteer for their latest cause.

Millennials Demand Work Life/Balance.

A standard 9-to-5 job is out of the question for millennials. In addition to time off for volunteer work, millennials need a fair balance between work and life in order to stay engaged. This desire translates to either flexible working hours or the ability to work from home. They are willing to work hard, but a standard 9-to-5 job is out of the question.

Millennials Are Social Creatures Who Need a Collaborative Work Environment.

Working from home is an excellent perk, but millennials do not want to work from home 100 percent of the time. They also crave collaboration with their peers (see Chapter 7). They are social creatures who want to feel a connection with their colleagues.

Millennials Are Impatient for Career Promotions.
Accustomed to instant gratification, they need recognition in
the form of quick promotions. They feel entitled to move up
the corporate ladder quickly. The standard two-year wait is
old-school thinking that won't work for millennials.

*Millennials Are Not as Money-Driven as Their Older
Colleagues.* They are willing to accept lower pay if it means
that some, preferably all, of the above criteria are met. So goes
the stereotype: high expectations, long list of demands, and low
tolerance for doing it the old way.

Origins of the Stereotype

The Perceived Need for Recognition

Millennials are thought to be recognition-hungry, praise-
mongers who need continuing acclaim. This stereotype is based
on a cascading waterfall of stereotypical generalizations that
goes back several lifetimes.

Today's millennials were raised by the often-ridiculed "helicopter" generation X parents. When generation X members were
young, so the story goes, their baby boomer parents were getting
divorced. (This was the peak baby boomer divorce years of the
1970s and 1980s.) In addition, baby boomer mothers were entering the workforce in record numbers. Therefore, it is surmised
that generation X was the least-parented generation in history.
Because baby-boomer women were not at home to take care of
their children, generation X toddlers often were sent to daycare
centers and later came home from school to empty homes.
This led to the stereotypical latchkey kid: a child neglected
and alone.

This experience supposedly traumatized generation X, and they collectively vowed never to raise their children in like circumstances. But, in yet another media-built stereotype, generation X parents became overprotective, overinvolved, overindulgent parents of the millennial generation.

Millennials were supposedly showered with praise by their helicopter parents (so named because, like helicopters, they hover). Self-esteem became a major concern during this period, so children were protected from any instance in which their self-esteem might be negatively affected. They were often given participation prizes: a ribbon at every sporting event, regardless of performance, and flowers at the finale. Helicopter parents often believed that declaring winners and losers was a cruel punishment for their less-athletic, less-talented children. Participation trophies and constant praise became a norm that continued into the workplace. As managers metaphorically replaced parents in a workplace setting, they, too, were expected to deliver the goods. However, instead of participation prizes, they were given plastic awards; and, instead of a merit badges, they expected raises and promotions. So say the gen-experts.

None of these assumptions are well-researched, and many are media driven. Many articles, in fact, contradict themselves regarding millennials' need for recognition. For example, one article (Smith, 2014) features the opinion expressed by a high-tech cloud company executive who asked this question: Do millennials really require *positive* feedback or do they simply have the natural human desire for any feedback? The simpler truth might be that millennials want to know how they are doing: Are they meeting expectations? Can they do better?

Another corporate blog (O'Donnell, 2015) suggests that the millennial employee problem is one of miscommunication. The blogger argues that millennials, having been raised with minimal criticism, exaggerate any corrective feedback as overly negative. Perhaps they just require constant positive recognition to balance exaggerated good with perceived bad. This also points to a supposed cause of intergenerational conflict among the generations: Older employees view younger employees' need for praise as a weakness that creates tension among employees.

The Perceived Need for Meaningful Work

Many articles have been written describing millennials' need to engage in meaningful work, including such titles as, *What Millennials Want Most: A Career That Actually Matters* (Salzsberg, 2012); *How to Become a Place Where Millennials Want to Work* (Salveopartners.com); *Millennials Want to Do Something That Is Meaningful, says Author Jamie Notter* (Mehra, 2015). These authors argue that millennials are not satisfied to simply punch a timecard; they want to make a difference. And they will not fully commit to a task, unless they understand how they are adding value. This is supposedly a result of two generational dynamics: the aforementioned helicopter parenting plus technology.

Helicopter Parenting. The same "blame the parents" attitude discussed in the previous section applies here. At the same time these parents were praising their children for a job well done—or any job at all, well done or not—they were also telling their children that they were very, very special. These overinvolved, overindulgent parents, it is argued, wanted their children to know how valuable they were, and the children believed them. Later, therefore, as they moved into the workplace, they felt the need to add value: to feel engaged in meaningful, important work. Feeling unimportant goes against everything they have known.

Technology. The second perceived reason millennials want meaningful work is their exposure to technology. They are not consumers of media, but creators of media, so the story goes.

They grew up creating and sharing content online. Because they grew up as the creators of culture, they feel the responsibility of creating meaningful content in their workplace.

However, the reality is that technology use among young people varies considerably. A study by Neil Selwyn (2009) of the University of London, titled *The Digital Native—Myth and Reality*, states that young people's ability to access technology remains strongly associated with economic status and social class. In addition, he quotes many surveys that reveal that most young people use technology for more passive media consumption, rather than for content creation in collaborative communities (as often described).

The myth that millennials want meaningful work because they were told they were special and grew up using collaborative technology is a stereotype, perpetuated by the media, and not based on research.

The Perceived Notion That Millennials Are Driven to Make the World a Better Place

As previously described, one of the most defining characteristics of the millennial stereotype is their drive to change the world. Millennials, so it goes, are uniquely positioned to change the world and must work for a company that also wants to make a difference. Business leaders are often counseled to align their business with some cause, specifically in order to keep their employees engaged and to recruit more millennials to the company.

Three factors drive this supposed need: racial diversity of the generation, increased accessibility of breaking news via social media, and the historical shifts with which our society has grappled during the generation's upbringing (gay rights, climate change, etc.).

Diversity. Millennials are the most diverse generation in U.S. history. In 2014, Pew Research Center tabulated that 43 percent of millennials in America were nonwhite. Therefore, one gen-expert argued, since millennials grew up with diversity, they have found unity in their uniqueness. This "unity in diversity" drives the equality-conscious mindset of millennials. They fight for equal rights, for the safety of all, tolerance, and freedom, and so forth. But is this unique to millennials?

News Junkies. It is said that millennials are also driven to change the world because breaking news is constantly at their fingertips. Even though Pew Research Center found that millennials do use social networking and the Internet at higher rates than any other generation, another misguided conclusion is drawn: Since millennials are bombarded with the horrors of attention-grabbing news headlines, confronted with social tragedies, injustice, images of stranded polar bears, and international conflict, they are drawn to right these injustices. They cannot simply ignore what they are seeing. But is this unique to millennials?

Historical Shifts. Finally, millennials are thought to have grown up in a time when significant social change has occurred beyond what generation X and baby boomers experienced. Millennials grew up during a time of climate change, gay-rights debate, immigration reform, international genocide, the rise of terrorism, and the war on drugs. Marketing campaigns for nonprofits have been telling millennials that they can make a difference, and millennials believe they can. Smokey Bear told millennials, "Only you can prevent forest fires," and McGruff, the Crime Dog, told the toddlers to "take a bite out of crime." Campaigns like these have ingrained a sense of responsibility in millennials that drives them to make a difference. But is this unique to millennials?

The Perception of the Need for Work/Life Balance

Another stereotype associated with the millennial workforce is their need for reasonable work/life balance. Countless articles advise managers to be aware of this need in order to keep their millennials engaged. However these articles contain numerous false assumptions: (1) millennials are lazy, have always been lazy, and need work/life balance because they want to have it all. (2) millennials need work/life balance so they can pursue their many passions outside of work. (3) millennials' comfort with technology makes working from home an expectation, not a perk. Let's look at these generalizations individually:

Lazy.   Many experts consider millennials to be the laziest generation. When millennials are portrayed in this light, the laziness is almost always associated with their lethargic childhood. When gen Xers and baby boomers were children, they played in the streets with their friends from the neighborhood. They would bike around town, build tree houses in the woods, and come home in time for dinner. Their parents rarely worried where they might be.

Millennials, however, grew up in different circumstances, so the gen-experts say. As the streets of America became more dangerous, millennials were restricted to supervised playdates in the home. Mostly, they played video games. Their addiction to technology meant they hated the outdoors and exercise. As they entered the workforce, their lethargic, lazy habits translated to a poor work ethic. Those who argue for this stereotype say that millennials' need for work/life balance is apparently motivated by a desire to go home and play *World of Warcraft*.

Passion Project.   Others argue that millennials are the antithesis of lazy. They desire work/life balance to pursue passion projects. This stereotype is often associated with the concept that millennials want to change the world. Authors suggest that managers give millennials time off in order to volunteer. This advice advances two stereotypes: time off work to make a difference creates happy, motivated millennial employees.

Most frustrating about these myths are the contradictions. While certain authors argue that millennials are lazy and unmotivated, others argue that they are driven to work on passion projects. Which one is it? Or could it be that degree of motivation depends on the person?

Technology.   Finally, the desire for work/life balance is also associated with millennials' comfort with technology. Because millennials grew up as digital natives, they have used technology to learn, to play, to socialize, and to study. As a result, they feel just as comfortable working online as they do at the office. Because they are always online, they can work from anyplace at any time. The stereotype, then, exhorts managers to give millennials freedom to work wherever they want, whenever they want. However, are older generations not familiar enough with technology to also work from home? Is this truly unique to millennials?

The Perception That Millennials Require a Collaborative Work Environment

Gen-experts also argue that creating a collaborative work environment is crucial to motivating millennials. This perception is supposedly fueled by two factors: technology and diversity.

Technology.   That millennials need to engage in a collaborative work environment is supposedly a result of the all-encompassing presence of game technology in their lives. They have grown up in virtual collaboration with peers all over the world, and they want to feed off each other in the workplace as well. Their tendency to collaborate is also tied to their addiction to sharing all manner of personal information online. It is assumed that since millennials spent their formative years using social media, they are comfortable sharing information—even in their business environments. Working in isolation is unacceptable for millennials who would rather leave their job than work alone, so say the gen-experts.

Diversity. Millennials are also said to be effective collaborators because they grew up as the most racially diverse generation. Being surrounded by diverse ethnicities and races supposedly translates to an appreciation for differences and opposing views, resulting in a more open mind when interacting with colleagues in the workplace.

However, research shows that collaboration is a workplace dynamic that all generations crave at some level. The IBM Institute for Business Values' Millennial Survey 2014 asked the collaboration question of 1,784 employees at numerous organizations in 12 countries. The respondents represented individuals from three generations. When asked about collaboration, 56 percent, or about half of millennials, said that they make better decisions when a variety of people provide input. Can this truly define the generation when only about half agree? It seems even less likely when one considers that generation Xers, in the same survey, agreed at a rate of 64 percent. So, according to the survey, gen Xers are more collaborative than millennials. One must be careful not to create another stereotype about generation X, however. Simply notice that generalizations do not always hold true.

The Perception Regarding Opportunities for Advancement

Finally, companies are warned that career advancement is a crucial motivational factor for millennials; they expect frequent promotions and shortcuts to the top. However, the warning adds, money is not their end game. In fact, they are happy to take lower pay if it means greater opportunities for advancement. This need is due to their entitled upbringing and their need for instant gratification.

Entitled. Millennials are portrayed as an entitled, unrealistic bunch. They are said to be self-centered, spoiled, and unreasonable. Because their parents told them they were special when they were young, they now believe they are not only unique, but highly skilled. Unfortunately for managers, the newly hired millennial will soon feel he or she could be doing the manager's job as well or better. The stereotype adds that millennials overestimate their skills and their value to an organization. And, if managers want to retain their millennial employees, they will have to reward millennials with artificial title bumps and clear career paths to the top.

But research shows that this is not always the case. The IBM study mentioned earlier also asked participants about recognition and praise. The generation X employees in the study were more likely to favor prizes and recognition for the work they have done than millennials.

Instant Gratification. Millennials grew up in the world of instant gratification. Technology facilitated instant information sharing. The patience associated with paying one's dues in the workplace is an unnecessary, old-fashioned concept to millennials who feel they should be rewarded the moment they exhibit good work. Whereas baby boomers would receive letters in the mail once a day, millennials are texting with all of their friends, all day. Whereas baby boomers had to visit the library to research a simple curiosity, millennials can ask Siri for an instant response. This dynamic supposedly fuels the impatient need to advance quickly in an organization.

Are older generations also not accustomed to instant gratification associated with modern-day technology? Have baby boomers not adapted to the fact that they can get mail more than once a day now? Could it be that desire to advance in an organization is a natural human drive associated with many generations? Could it not also be that many millennials are simply not as concerned with advancement?

The Perception Involving Compensation

Until recently, financial reward was the primary, if not only, motivation for employees to work. Now, the myth is that millennials have higher expectations. Compensation is just one piece of the incentive puzzle for them. Managers are told that millennials look for all of the aforementioned criteria before worrying about salary. Money is almost a nonfactor in motivating millennials. Unlike their money-hungry, gen X and baby boomer colleagues, millennials are more likely to stay in a low-paying job if they have the above requirements met—including constant praise and recognition, meaningful work, the opportunity to change the world, work/life balance, and a collaborative work environment. In addition, their need for career development opportunities is fueled more by a desire for validation than the associated pay increase.

The Truth about Motivating Millennials

General assumptions concerning the millennial generation found in the corporate literature and business journals, seminars, and newspaper articles can be very persuasive. However, implicit in these generalizations is the contrasting assumption that generation X and baby-boomer employees do not value these things as much or, indeed, at all. Research indicates that the assumptions are false. The IBM Institute for Business Value Millennial Survey 2014 asked members of each generation which attributes an organization must offer to help employees feel motivated at work. Participants were asked to select their top three choices from a list that included inspirational leadership, clearly articulated vision/business strategy, work/life balance and flexibility, performance-based recognition and promotions, freedom to innovate, and a collaborative work environment. The results indicated that distribution across all three generations varied very little.

These findings indicate that there are few differences among generations regarding their desire for accolades, their need for work/life balance, or their interest in a collaborative work environment.

Other studies contradict the stereotypes as well. A 2010 study published in the *Journal of Management* (Schullery, 2013) compared surveys from more than 16,000 high school seniors. The surveys were taken in 1976 (baby boomers), 1991 (gen Xers), and 2006 (millennials). The participants were asked to rate importance of work values. By and large, the study revealed no significant differences.

I have heard the argument that generational studies do not perpetuate stereotype but rather examine trends in society's cultural shifts. I appreciate the study of trends, but placing large groups of people into buckets based on these trends is a dangerous practice in the workplace, even when well-intentioned. The consequences of these erroneous perceptions can have major effects in a business environment.

A friend of mine recently shared a story about how generational labels resulted in unintended consequences within her small, California-based service organization. The woman worked in human resources and was at an annual meeting for more than 300 sales and services employees in the organization. The CEO kicked off the three-day session with a rousing speech about how the company was committed to high working standards in order to motivate all employees. He announced that he had been researching how to engage his employees and proudly said that, convinced by his extensive study on the subject, he was persuaded that each generation was motivated by different values. "Millennials these days are not as motivated by money," he said. "In fact, they value work/life balance much more."

This seemingly harmless comment sparked alarm among the millennials and the older generations as well. Over the course of the next three days, numerous employees reached out to my friend in HR for a meeting. Overwhelmingly, the millennials had questions about their compensation and whether they were being paid fairly. They assumed, upon hearing the CEO's speech, that they might be able to get a bigger paycheck if they weren't quite so "millennial." Perhaps they might give up a little on work/life balance and get a raise in salary. The older workers who reached out to my friend had complaints too. They argued that they, too, had a need for work/life balance. One director said she would trade pay for vacation days in a heartbeat.

It is possible that some, perhaps even most, millennials in that organization valued work/life balance over money, but making the sweeping generalization, based on the faulty research commonly found in business media, created exactly the confusion, resentment, and concern one would expect. Using the generational labels to describe this phenomenon was divisive in this workplace. Even though the factors listed earlier, such as work/life balance and compensation, are crucial tools in a manager's toolkit for motivating and engaging employees, associating these tools with any single generation does not benefit the organization. In fact, it hurts.

Overcoming the Stereotypes

The primary responsibilities for managers is employee engagement. In order to motivate your team effectively, remember that there is no one-size-fits-all approach. Your team is made up of individuals, not stereotypes; an effective manager must understand what drives each person. What works for one employee may not work for another. The following are tips for managers to engage their employees, regardless of generation.

Evaluate Motivational Factors Most Important to Each of Your Team Members

Motivating employees can be a challenge. Even though managers have a seemingly endless list of tools to engage employees, selecting the best options for a team can be tricky. The list of tools in this chapter, such as compensation and work/life balance, represents only a part of the motivational tools. Other tools include providing an optimum work environment and physical space; opportunities for learning, development, and innovation; and performance feedback, to name just a few.

Psychologist Abraham Maslow's 1954 book on *Motivation and Personality* contains Maslow's Hierarchy of Needs, which became the widely accepted model for understanding human motivation. His model lists five levels of needs for human self-actualization: physiological needs, safety, love/belonging, esteem, and, finally, self-actualization.

Although the theory is typically interpreted as a rigid hierarchy (such that a person cannot move to the next level of needs without satisfying the requirements listed in the previous level), Maslow wrote that need fulfillment does not always follow the same progression. For example, one person may have a higher need for love than self-esteem, whereas the need for creativity (self-actualization) may supersede basic physiological needs for some others. This model is useful in brainstorming the five types of tools at your disposal for employee engagement. Discuss with your team their priorities, and draw on your toolkit for creative ways to meet their needs. Below are some suggestions:

Physiological. The first level of Maslow's Hierarchy of Needs is physiological. Physiological needs include breathing, food, water, sex, and sleep, for example. Many motivational tools fall into this category, the most obvious being compensation. Employees need enough money to buy food. Also, if the need for work/life balance is motivated by the need for rest, it also falls in this category.

Brainstorm ways to motivate your team such as:

- Compensation: Offer your employees secure compensation in ways other than a straight paycheck, such as services, meal plans, and so forth.
- Work/life balance: As a manager, are you more focused on the number of hours that your employees work than on the results they achieve? Evaluate whether you are watching the clock to a fault and how you can ensure goals are accomplished, even if employees aren't putting in a full 40-hour week.
- Flexible working hours: Does your global team take late-night or early-morning calls? Consider giving them extra time off to offset the lost sleep.
- Breaks: One company implemented a 10 a.m. and 2 p.m. stretch break for all employees. Getting people out of their seats together encouraged social conversation and boosted employee morale.
- Rest areas: Some Silicon Valley companies have installed nap rooms in their office for employees who need a midday snooze. This may be one way to offset employee burnout.

Safety. This level describes not only physical safety, which should be a top priority for managers, but also employees' need for security. Security includes emotional well-being, as well as a safe place to work. Knowing they can rely on their employment for the long term can give employees a sense of ongoing security for their physiological needs, as well as for their health, property, and family.

Brainstorm ways to motivate your team such as:

- Health and Safety: Monitor and enforce good health and safety practices.
- Show Concern: Knowing that management is concerned for safety allows employees to be less distracted, more trusting, and less stressed. Think of authentic ways to demonstrate that you, as a manager, care.
- Secure Employment: Knowing that a company is financially solvent offers a sense of long-term employment security. If possible, inform your employees about the company's long-term sustainability.
- Job Security: Ensure that employees know that their job is not at risk. Treat mistakes as learning opportunities and encourage employees to correct the error and try again.
- Benefits: Health benefits and retirement benefits offer a sense of security for employees, their families, and their future financial situation.

Love/Belonging. Love/belonging includes the need for social affiliation. A collaborative working environment creates a sense of belonging. Caring for your employees beyond the day-to-day tasks can help them feel they are valued as part of a community. Rewards such as acknowledging an employee's good work can also satisfy this social need.

Brainstorm ways to motivate your team, such as:

- Collaborative work environment: Facilitate cooperative teamwork, not only because it is good business practice, but also because it allows your employees to feel they are a part of something larger than themselves. Ensure that this is a value for all employees, not just millennials.
- Personal relationships: Ensure that your team connects at a personal level in order to foster a sense of belonging within the team. This can be done informally or through regular team-building workshops.
- Work/life balance: Think of ways to promote work/life balance so that employees are able to spend optimum time with friends and family.
- Accessibility: Be accessible to your employees with either an open-door policy or with regular check-ins. Knowing that you are available increases employee motivation.
- Role Model: As the leader, your behavior will likely be mirrored in the workplace. Be kind and connect with people. Your team will be more likely to do the same among themselves.

Esteem. The fourth level describes the feeling that one is secure in oneself, that life is meaningful and purposeful. The desire for meaningful work can fall into this category and is not limited to millennials. Encouragement and praise also fall into this category. Public acknowledgment lets employees know that they are respected by others and offers them a sense of achievement. However, some employees abhor the attention that comes with public acknowledgment, so be aware of individual preferences.

Brainstorm ways to motivate your employees such as:

- Meaningful Work: One simple but often-overlooked tactic for managers is to ensure that employees understand the company's vision and strategy. By connecting the dots between the company's mission and their own, employees can see clearly how they add value.
- Goals: Set realistic and clear goals so that employees feel a sense of achievement when they hit their targets.
- Recognition: Grant prizes and awards for outstanding performance. This promotes admiration and attention from the team.
- Encouragement and Praise: Offering regular encouragement and praise is one free way to award accomplishment and boost employees' self-worth.
- Balance feedback: Encouragement and praise without constructive feedback can result in overcomplimenting and can seem inauthentic. Ensure that you balance praise with constructive feedback in order to create balance.
- Promotions: Offer promotions and additional responsibilities when earned to demonstrate that your employees are valued.

Self-Actualization. Finally, self-actualization refers to people's motivation to reach their own full potential. If managers are meeting employees' expectations at all other levels of motivation, then this, too, can be achieved. This is the ultimate goal and is specific to the individual. For example, perhaps self-actualization is the ability to make a difference in the world for one employee, whereas accomplishing meaningful work is the end goal for another. Again, it is crucial to have conversations with your employees to understand their needs and motivations.

Maslow wrote that only 2 percent of the population reaches this state of self-actualization.

If your employees are at least on the path, then brainstorm ways to be part of their process, such as:

- Journey: Focus on the journey, not the end game, and appreciate the difficult path that your employees are following in order to grow. This places emphasis on the individual as they work toward the end goal.
- Challenging Work: Offer your employees career-stretching assignments and challenging work in order to facilitate their growth.
- Decision Making: Invite employees at this level to be part of the decision-making process, as their contributions may be valuable assets to your management team.
- Autonomy: Give employees appropriate autonomy because their solutions may be better than you had imagined.
- Learn from them: Every employee has something to offer, and you can learn from your employees as much, if not more, than they learn from you. Look for opportunities to expand your understanding through your team.

Beware of Your Own Biases

As a manager, you are also an employee yourself and have your own set of motivations and needs. This may influence your perspective on what is important to your employees. Although personal experience can be a powerful tool as a manager, it can also be a hindrance to true understanding. For example, imagine if your company had implemented an employee engagement survey and that you found that work/life balance was very important to many of your employees. Because balance is also important to you, you decide to implement work-from-home Fridays. You may feel you are being sensitive to your employees' needs and motivating them appropriately. However, this might not be the case!

Work/life balance can mean many things to many people, as one survey revealed. This study, one of the most comprehensive meta-studies on generational issues ever conducted, was done by Universum, an employer-branding firm, working in partnership with INSEAD Emerging Market Institute and The HEAD foundation. They surveyed more than 16,000 millennials in 43 countries on a number of work-related issues and published their findings in a six-part series. One question—"What does work/life balance mean to you?"—elicited responses such as "enough leisure time for my private life," "recognition and respect for the employees," and "convenient work location." Answers varied by region, as well. For example, "convenient work location" was prized more heavily in Central and Eastern Europe than in the Middle East.

Therefore, when the hypothetical employee engagement survey, cited as an example earlier, revealed that employees wanted more work/life balance, working from home on Fridays may or may not have addressed that need. It could have meant that the team was looking for a more convenient work location.

It is important, then, to discuss in detail what engages your employees to ensure the best working environment for your team. You might even consider holding a focus group with your team to gather their input. Ask your colleagues what has worked for them. Take on a coach or mentor to discuss how you can best manage the team based on their needs. Question your own assumptions as much as possible to ensure you are not unknowingly trapped in your own biases.

Check in Regularly with Each Team Member to Assess if Things Have Changed

As well as evaluating engagement of your team members, be on the lookout for warning signs that your employees may be becoming disengaged. What worked in the past may no longer be successful. Check for an increase in sickness, absenteeism, or tardiness. A shift in quality of work may also indicate a problem. Finally, if an employee is communicating with you less or seems to have a shift in attitude, it is time to check in.

As a manager, you already might be initiating in-depth discussions about motivation and engagement. This is a good thing! However, remember not to fall into the trap of putting your employees in a box regarding their attitudes and leaving them there. Priorities change. Check in with your employee every six months to ensure that their needs have not shifted. Life circumstances, values, and preferences can be fluid.

Take Stock of Your Strengths and Weaknesses in Engaging Your Team

Reassessing your strengths and weaknesses periodically to understand where you might improve is important. Consider a 360-degree evaluation. It is a good way for a manager to receive feedback from managers, peers, employees, and, potentially, customers. A number of vendors offer to facilitate 360-degree evaluations, and there is even some software available. The evaluation is a powerful tool for understanding your blind spots. Take advantage of the 360-degree evaluation if your company offers this kind of assessment.

Illusory superiority (also known as the above-average effect) is a cognitive bias in which individuals overestimate their own qualities and abilities relative to others. This applies to their performance on tasks, as well as to assessing their level of desirable characteristics. Research shows that this bias also may apply to managers and their leadership style.

The IBM study cited earlier in the chapter asked leaders how well they were doing in recognizing their workers' accomplishments. They also asked the workers for their opinion on how well their manager was doing in this role. Every generation of work-ers rated their leader's ability to recognize their accomplishments lower than the leaders rated themselves in their role.

The same study also asked employees about the attributes of a perfect manager. Themes across all generations included being ethical, fair, dependable, consistent, and transparent. Remember that motivational factors are not the only skills you have in your toolbox as a manager.

Summary

The Stereotype: Millennials are different from other genera-tions because they need more recognition and praise, need to be doing "meaningful" work, are interested in changing the world, demand work/life balance, prefer a collaborative work environment, and need obvious opportunities for advancement. They are less interested in high compensation if these needs are met.

The Truth: What engages millennials is not significantly different from what engages members of other generations. Indi-vidual millennials are motivated by individual preferences.

What a manager should do about it: Ignore the stereotypes and embrace the individuality of your team members. Here are four steps to help you do so:

1. Evaluate what motivational factors are most important to each of your team members.
2. Beware of your own biases.
3. Check in regularly with each team member to assess if things have changed.
4. Take stock of your own strengths and weaknesses in moti-vating your team.

6

Performance Management

P erformance management refers to how a manager plans, reviews, and develops employees' performance. This chapter will identify generational assumptions, as demonstrated by the millennial stereotype, pertaining to performance management.

The Stereotype

Cassie is a stereotypical millennial. She needs significant hand-holding because her work ethic is not strong. She questions every assignment given her, incessantly asking the purpose of the assignment. She requires a lot of feedback on the work she produces (much more feedback than older employees require). She is also demanding about professional development opportunities. She expects the company to invest heavily in training to help her advance. In short, Cassie is a handful!

Advice on how to manage the performance of millennials is not in short supply. Managers often consider millennials one of the most high-maintenance generations in the workforce. This chapter will address ill-conceived advice regarding planning, reviewing, and developing millennial performance, as well as the stereotypes on which this advice is based. Finally, included is a review of performance management best practices regardless of generation. First we review the stereotypes:

Performance Planning
- Millennials have a poor work ethic so they are in need of clear direction and supervision.
- Millennials insist on efficiency, so they are constantly asking "why," hoping to eliminate unnecessary processes.
- Millennials need to understand how they are adding value to the company in order to feel motivated.

Performance Reviewing

- Millennials demand timely and consistent feedback.
- When millennials are not given enough encouragement, they do not feel they are adequately appreciated.
- In order to deliver negative feedback to millennials, managers must first adorn them with numerous positive affirmations, or millennials will shut down.

Performance Development

- Personal and professional development is a higher priority for millennials than for other generations.
- Performance development in the form of training and mentoring is considered a right, not a privilege.
- Incorporating technology into learning opportunities is crucial in order to keep millennials engaged in the learning.

If these assumptions were true, millennials would be a difficult challenge for any manager. In the next section, we will deal with each element in more depth, the origin of the assumption, and the reason the assumption is flawed.

Performance Planning

Millennials Have a Poor Work Ethic, so They Need Clear Direction and Supervision. Millennials' poor work ethic is said to result from their lethargic childhood. As previously described and in contrast to gen Xers and baby boomers, millenials were restricted to supervised playdates in the home. Their world was restricted by the perceived dangers outside the home and the overbearing parents inside. These restrictions explain their familiarity with video games. Their addiction to technology, in turn, meant they were resistant to the outdoors and exercise. As they entered the workforce, their lethargic, lazy habits translated to a poor work ethic. However, because they were born into an affluent, easy life, they probably did not have to work much in high school and spent very few hours studying in college. The 40-hour work week, therefore, is considered foreign and uncomfortable for this generation.

To manage an employee of this nature, managers are advised essentially to micromanage. Since millennials have neither the experience nor the motivation to self-manage, they will need their manager's constant hand-holding. Left to their own devices (pun intended), millennials will be facebooking, tweeting, redditing rebels, distracted from work by nonstop cell-phone notifications.

Millennials Insist on Efficiency, so They Are Constantly Asking "Why," Hoping to Identify and Eliminate Unnecessary Processes. As millennials were growing up, they saw technology become faster, smaller, more powerful, and more efficient. This need for speed and efficiency is a byproduct of being what is commonly referred to as a "digital native" (being born and raised in a time of digital technology). Fully aware of their technological prowess, millennials are perceived to be denigrating older generations, who seem to be less interested in efficiency and more invested in the way things have always been done. Therefore, some authors conclude, millennials naturally and continually question the way things have always been done, because they are convinced they can find a better way.

Millennials seem to have no patience for bureaucracy, red tape, extra steps, or hoops to jump through. Faced with what they perceive as useless extra work, they will rebel. Managers, therefore, need to explain relevance at every step.

Despite their lack of experience, millennials cannot sit quietly with their thoughts. They do not have the patience to watch and learn. Instead they will constantly be asking "why?" Managers are advised to be prepared with answers or risk getting stuck with millennials who roll their eyes and "check out".

Millennials Need to Understand How They Are Adding Value to the Company. This generation, we are told, was raised by overbearing, overprotective parents. They were rewarded even for little effort, praised for insignificant achievements, and reminded often how special they were. Therefore, as the millennials move into the workplace, they want to continue feeling that they are important to the process. Many articles describe how millennials crave meaningful work, that they are not satisfied simply to punch a timecard, and that they resent busywork. Therefore, they will not fully and happily commit to a task unless they first understand how they are adding value. Managers are told not to expect easy compliance but to be prepared with explanations and justifications. Gen-experts write that feeling unimportant goes against everything millennials have ever known.

Performance Reviewing

Millennials Demand Timely and Consistent Feedback on a Continuous Basis. The perception that millennials demand consistent and timely feedback is a result of the instant-gratification stereotype. The label "digital natives" results from millennials being associated with today's fast-moving barrage of data: comments, likes, replies, retweets, and other digital feedback. When individuals post an image, a comment, or a video, they are broadcasting that content to a massive, global community. Within seconds they can receive validation or criticism from their peers on the nature of that content.

That expectation is then transferred to the manager in the work-place. Managers are advised to stay in constant communication with their millennial employees. For example, many articles have been written denouncing the "ineffective" practice of holding biannual performance reviews. Receiving feedback from a manager only twice a year will not suffice, the articles state. In fact, managers are cautioned that if millennials do not receive regular feedback, they are at a high risk of leaving, making this a crucial tip for managers hoping to retain millennial talent.

Millennials Need Encouragement to Feel Adequately Appreciated. Not only were the so-called helicopter parents overindulgent of their children's egos, they also, supposedly, had unreasonably high expectations. As a result, they provided their millennial children with constant feedback in an effort to support their development and growth. Growing up in a supportive family that provides such feedback and encouragement could theoretically create a similar need in the workplace. In fact, we are told, millennials expect this kind of coaching and encouragement in order to replicate the family dynamic.

Amplifying the stereotype is the idea that millennials do not view their managers as experts in technology or content. Growing up online, with the ability to Google almost any subject at any time, millennials are said to feel that they are experts in all fields. Why would they need a manager's technical knowledge if they can use any number of websites to learn quickly the same information? Instead, millennials expect managers to act more as coaches and mentors, whose primary role is to provide encouragement and support. If millennials do not have that relationship with their managers, they might feel underappreciated.

Further heightening the stakes, some articles describe how older generations perceive this need for encouragement as needy and selfish. In contrast, having spent their careers not being told as often that they were special, baby boomers and gen Xers are said to resent the neediness of this newest generation. This is often the cause of intergenerational conflict.

Millennials Require Numerous Positive Comments Before Negative Feedback. Once again, this stereotype blames millennial expectations on the influence of social media. Social media engines serve as conduits for sharing information about one's life with the world. As a result, Facebook and Twitter are accused of creating a youth culture of "digital narcissism." Narcissism is defined as having excessive interest in oneself and/or an inflated sense of importance. Many managers consider their millennials to be far more narcissistic than their older peers. Logically, if millennials were truly narcissistic, they would require significant attention and feedback from their managers. Consequently, providing constructive criticism might be difficult, if not risky.

Some experts argue that millennials are so uncomfortable with negative feedback that they perceive it as an actual attack, and when millennials are attacked, their defenses are raised. The millennial focuses more on the attack than on what is said. Therefore, a millennial might not hear what is being said, missing the valuable guidance a manager might be offering. Managers are advised, then, to shower millennials with excessive positive affirmations in order to counterbalance any negative feedback. This praise and appreciation will supposedly create a relationship in which millennials are less likely to shut down when receiving negative feedback.

Performance Development

Personal and Professional Development Is a Higher Priority for Millennials. Expectations for educational attainment have changed in the last 50 years. Whereas the silent generation could create a respectable career with only a high school diploma, today's generation needs a higher education. As baby boomers and gen Xers watched this shift occur throughout their lifetime, they are said to have reared their children to believe that education is the path to success. That value, if true, would create a generation of consumer students. Although millennials are believed to place high importance on learning and development opportunities, older generations are described as not so consumed with this desire to learn. As a result, managers are counseled that millennials will be unsatisfied if they are not given ample development opportunities. They have an ingrained need to continue their studies.

Technology also plays a role in this stereotype. Millennials have long been accustomed to a deluge of information. The Internet is a never-ending stream of thoughts, perspectives, facts, and resources. Growing up in the information age results in millennials viewing life as a learning experience. Managers are advised that the learning experience for millennials must not stop in the workplace.

Performance Development in the Form of Training and Mentoring Is Considered a Right. Another perception about millennials involves their hunger for advancement (discussed in depth in Chapter 5). This so-called narcissistic generation expects to advance quickly within their organization and would rather not pay their proverbial dues. Aware of the need to increase their skills in order to advance, millennials consider training and mentoring a necessity and right, not a perk. Not providing development options has been described as a slap in the face to millennials. *Development* is defined as training and mentoring, but also includes career-stretching assignments, conferences, and networking opportunities. Millennials view these formal and informal learning tools as the responsibility of their employers. By not offering these opportunities, the companies are allowing their greatest asset (millennials, presumably) to stagnate.

Incorporating Technology into Learning Opportunities Is Crucial to Keep Millennials Engaged in the Learning. Many stereotypes associated with millennials stem from the notion that they are digital natives. Consumed with technology in every aspect of their lives, they are often called tech addicts who suffer withdrawal pains when away from their cell phones. These Internet-connected youth are considered active participants in Web 2.0 (referring to user-generated web content). No longer comfortable with the passive nature of traditional educational instruction, millennials want a fast-paced, collaborative workshop environment, supplied with advanced technology. Authors seem comfortable assuming that since millennials have been exposed to more technology in their lives than older generations, they must also want it more. This means managers are frequently advised to incorporate technology in the workplace, if only to satisfy their millennial employees. This must be especially true in corporate learning environments. Most of the time, the connection between childhood technology use and engagement with technology is assumed. As such, managers and trainers are urged to incorporate technology into their learning programs or risk losing millennials' attention.

The Truth about Managing Millennial Performance

Performance Planning

The myths around planning performance indicate that millennials have poor work ethic, need direction, constantly ask why, look to create efficiencies, and need to understand how they are adding value. In reality, these myths are almost impossible to substantiate. For example, in today's work culture, one cannot view the work ethic concept in the classic way. Imagine an employee who works from home in his bunny slippers, goes out to lunch with friends, then takes long breaks to walk his dog three times a day. However, when he wakes up in the morning, he responds to work emails before even sitting up in bed. He takes calls late at night to keep in touch with clients in India, and he works at least a few hours a day on weekends. He may also sometimes take an entire weekday off to go surfing, but will also work straight through the night on a pending project. Compare that to employees who work an eight-hour shift in an office, with a lunch hour and two scheduled breaks. They may work intensely while at their desk, even eating through lunch, but then they go home and completely disconnect. Who has a better work ethic? In today's work culture, the term is less easy to define. And most polls and questionnaires that ask about work ethic do not define it for the participants.

When a study published by the Pew Research Center (2010a) asked millennials if they felt they had as strong a work ethic as older generations, most respondents said no. However, the term *work ethic* was not defined for the participants. This was a self-assessment, not an objective behavioral analysis. Possibly, after years of being told they had poor work ethic, millennials believed it.

Lester, Standifer, Schultz, and Windsor (2012) published a paper that identified actual-versus-perceived differences in generations. The results revealed that perceived differences significantly outnumbered actual differences.

All three of the myths associated with performance planning seem to indicate that millennials need clear communication from managers about long- and short-term goals, organizational strategy, and how and where they fit into the big picture. The IBM Institute for Business Value (2014) surveyed 1,784 employees from numerous organizations in 12 countries and asked specifically about desire for clear direction, the need to understand the business strategy, and the desire to add value.

The results show that all generations across the board had similar attitudes, behavioral patterns, and values in the workplace. Does this mean that all people are the same? No, it means that members of each generation are equally diverse in their preferences. In essence, managers cannot anticipate employees' needs or preferences based on their generation.

Performance Review

In reviewing performance with millennials, the advice is to focus on feedback, praise, and encouragement. Once again, research shows that this is not more important for millennials than it is for other generations. The IBM survey cited earlier revealed that millennials were no hungrier for accolades than those of other generations. If anything, gen Xers were more inclined to want recognition for some qualities, such as collaboration and information sharing. However, by and large, the differences were not significant. Across the board, praise and encouragement were rated important by about half the population, indicating that no generation is particularly inclined (or disinclined) to rate this need high.

Focusing only on millennials, one finds significant differences within the millennial geographic range. For example, millennials in Africa were far more likely to desire feedback than millennials in other regions. Although three-quarters of millennials in Africa said feedback from managers was very important, only 40 percent of millennials in Central and Eastern Europe said the same. The North American response fell at approximately 50 percent. That means that if a manager in North America has two millennials on the team, odds are he might have one who strongly desires feedback and one who does not.

Some research studies claim to provide evidence that millennials require more managerial feedback than other generations. Managers must, however, be careful to distinguish between desiring and requiring feedback. Once such study, Workforce 2020, conducted by Oxford Economics for SAP in 2015, found that one-third of the millennials polled said they expected more feedback than they were currently receiving. According to the survey, more than two-thirds of millennials want feedback from their managers monthly. In the same survey, fewer than half the participants in the older generation responded that they expected feedback that often. Do the older generations not expect it because they have enough experience to know they will not get it? Or do they not expect it because they do not want it? And even if there is a disparity between preferences, on what basis should millennials be managed differently? Should desire for feedback be the determining factor in best practices for giving feedback? I desire chocolate cake every day but it is not best practice for me to eat it that often.

Performance Development

The professional development stereotypes associated with millennials indicate that they are consummate learners who crave technology-infused training opportunities. First, if millennials are insatiable learners, then how does that sit with the stereotype that they have a poor work ethic? Does the desire to learn and study not qualify as a work ethic? This is only one of many contradictions in generational assumptions. For example, some research has indicated that millennials have a lower desire to learn than other generations. A study by Laura Holyoke and Erick Larson (2009) published in the *Journal of Adult Education* measured readiness to learn, orientation to learn, and motivation to learn across generations. The results indicated that millennials had the lowest readiness to learn of any generation, citing distractions or a lack of curiosity as the main reasons. However, this study does not address the diversity within the population. The surveyed group consisted of

60 students enrolled in a graduate school class. Can conclusions be drawn without knowing what other environmental factors contributed to this finding? Can managers rely on data from such a narrow population?

Evidence is mixed regarding millennials' desire for incorporating more technology in a development program than other generations. A University of Central Florida study that surveyed 1,489 respondents revealed that older learners reported higher satisfaction with web-based learning than younger generations. Conversely, the IBM study previously cited showed that millennials were more comfortable with virtual learning than their older colleagues. And a study (Walker & Jorn, 2009) produced by the Office of Information Technology at the University of Minnesota on the twenty-first century student found no correlation between age and desire for technology in the classroom. My own peer-reviewed study also found no correlation. Which of these studies should we believe? It is more likely that a number of factors—such as region, organization, job level, nationality, gender, birth order, socioeconomic class, the number of televisions that were in their homes as children, the level of trauma experienced by individuals, or history of drug and alcohol abuse—were affecting the results seen in these populations. This is further evidence that managers should not make broad generalizations when anticipating the needs of their employees.

Overcoming the Stereotypes

Performance management is a crucial component of the manager-employee relationship. Managers have a responsibility to support their team in planning and setting expectations, reviewing performance over time, and developing an employee's skillset in the interest of professional and personal growth. As is typically the case, there is no perfect plan for performance management. Although there may be best practices, these do not apply to all individuals, in all situations. Some employees may require more support than others. Likewise, some employees may require more support in certain situations than in other situations.

Situational leadership, a model developed by Hersey, Blanchard, and Johnson (2012) in the 1970s, is based on the premise that the most effective leaders adjust their behavior based on individual employees or, even better, the task. For example, Lucy has just joined an organization as a Senior Manager of Product Marketing. She has more than 15 years of product-marketing experience but has never managed a team. In her new role, she will be leading the strategic direction for product marketing and will be managing a team of four people. The situational leadership model would suggest that Lucy's manager adapt his leadership style based on her experience and the present task. Lucy would likely need more guidance, feedback, and development when it comes to her management skills, and less guidance, feedback, and development in product marketing.

Managers must be flexible in their performance management and use an appropriate assessment to understand the most effective approach when dealing with team members. The flexible approach includes open conversations with employees, listening to their needs, understanding their motivations, and adapting a management style to each employee. Most important, the approach must include accepting employees individually and not applying a predetermined personality, based on generation.

With that backdrop, the following section contains key tips for effective management in the areas of planning, reviewing, and developing performance.

Performance Planning

Performance planning is the process of identifying and communicating expectations for each employee. The following are key tips:

Break Goals and Expectations into Two Categories: Results and Behavior. Results are the specific goals or deliverables against which an employee is measured; behaviors are the methods an employee demonstrates during the process. Not only must employees be clear on assigned goals, they also need to know how they are expected to achieve those goals.

Ensure goals are clear to employees by implementing George Doran's (1981) SMART (specific, measurable, attainable, relevant, and timely) objectives. When these objectives are implemented, goals can be fairly evaluated, leaving little ambiguity. The IBM study mentioned earlier found that all three generations cited fairness as an important attribute of the ideal manager.

Clearly identifying expected behaviors can be as important. Although these behaviors are more difficult to measure, identifying them gives employees an understanding of the company's culture and norms. For example, a trainer is given a SMART objective to deliver training to 300,000 employees by the end of the fiscal year. The company expects its trainer to work closely with the curriculum development department. However, the trainer prefers to do his own curriculum development and does not involve the department. He might hit his SMART objective, but his behavior is not what his manager expected. The expected employee behaviors are sometimes referred to as performance dimensions, values, or competencies.

Connect an Employee's Goals and Expectations to the Organization's. Effective organizations have overarching goals and a strategy to meet them. Connecting your employees' goals to the organization's goals has many benefits. Often referred to as "cascading" goals or strategy, the connection can benefit both the employee and the organization. First, alignment ensures that employees are working on projects that benefit the organization. Misalignment of goals can be costly. In addition, when employees understand how their contribution affects the organization as a whole, employee engagement improves.

The understanding must go beyond simple targets, however. For example, a salesperson has a target of $200,000 for the fiscal year and is told that the company's overarching target is $300 million. Technically, the employee has been told how his or her goal connects to the larger picture. However, more benefit is gained if the employee understands the product mix, the target market and strategy, and the reason $300 million is the overall target.

Reviewing Performance

Once expectations are set, managers are expected to review performance regularly with employees. The following are tips for reviewing performance:

Communicate Purpose and Value in the Review Process.
Because performance reviews can be unpleasant if employees feel they are being attacked, communicating the purpose and value of the review process is important. As a manager, communicate authentically that your goal is the betterment of the employee, as well as the company. Some managers take a policing role in performance reviews. This attitude can lead to mistrust between the employee and manager. Take stock of your personal motivations and feelings about your employees and ensure you are operating in their best interest. Have conversations with your employees to communicate your perspective and establish that you value their contributions.

Establish a Cadence That Works. At one extreme, managers review performance once a year during annual performance appraisals (if at all). At the other extreme, managers talk with employees at the end of every day. Determining the best cadence is situational and depends on employees, their role in the organization, their experience with various tasks, their preferences, the organizational culture, and agreements between employees and managers. Discuss the optimum frequency of performance reviews for both results and behaviors and agree on how to deal with unexpected circumstances that may require timely feedback. Because setting expectations takes the guesswork out of potentially uncomfortable conversations, have an honest conversation with each employee about company expectations. Although formal and informal performance reviews can be stressful, clearly defined timelines and ground rules can lessen the tension.

Promote a Feedback Culture. By promoting feedback from your team, you can normalize the potentially uncomfortable conversations inherent in performance reviews. One of the most effective ways to promote feedback is to model the behavior you desire. That means asking your team, your peers, and your manager for feedback on yourself. Being open to what you receive demonstrates the behavior you wish to see in your team.

Give Clear Feedback. Bracketing constructive feedback between two positive affirmations in order to ease the blow is often called the "feedback sandwich." Although this method can be less stressful from the manager's perspective, it is more confusing for the employee. Instead, consider separating positive and developmental feedback to create greater clarity. In order to do this effectively, managers must strike a balance between positive feedback and corrective feedback. This balance will leave employees more open to receive constructive feedback separately.

In addition, in order for feedback to be effective, it must be specific. Whether the feedback is positive or negative, give examples of the actual and desired behavior. Do not just say, "Good job." Instead, tell employees what they did that was effective. Conversely, explain how an employee's work may have negatively affected the organization and what specific improvements would benefit both the employee and the organization.

Developing Performance

Developing your employee's performance is the third piece of the performance management puzzle. The following are some tips for developing employee performance.

Create Development Goals. Development goals are different from the results and behavior goals discussed in the planning session. Although the manager often sets results and behavioral goals, development goals can be more employee-driven and go beyond the scope of the employee's job description. These are goals employees have set for their continued development, perhaps in anticipation of their next role. Establishing development goals may also indirectly improve an employee's job performance. The goals also facilitate conversation between the manager and employee about what motivates the employee.

Create Formal and Informal Development Opportunities. Employees have different motivational levels for development. The key for managers is to make numerous options available so that employees can take advantage of the learning that best suits them. Because managers often have minimal control over budget and resources for employee development, thinking creatively about development is important. Although formal learning, such as classroom or virtual training, can be beneficial, it can come at a cost. Formal training can greatly benefit your team and should be encouraged if the budget allows. However, numerous free, informal learning opportunities are available:

- Mentoring, either internal or external to the organization
- Social learning, including blogs, RSS feeds, and social platforms
- On-demand learning, such as podcasts and other digital content

Also, on-the-job learning opportunities, such as rotational assignments, special projects, and job shadowing, should be offered.

Give Employees Visibility into Your Organization's Operations. Learning more about the business beyond their role can be a development opportunity for employees. By sharing in the organization's direction, employees can expand their understanding beyond their own contributions. Learning about challenges, such as changing customer expectations, industry trends, and the economic climate, helps employees contribute more beneficially to the organization. To encourage their involvement, invite them to brainstorm, ask questions, and offer recommendations. The involvement will offer employees a broader base of understanding from which to select their own development goals.

Avoid Labels That Create Divisions. Some of the aforementioned managerial suggestions mirror those in the literature that legitimizes the concept of generational differences. I take no issue with giving millennials feedback, for example. However, the problems with these articles are twofold:

1. They cause divisiveness by excluding older generations, as if these recommendations do not apply to them.
2. They oversimplify the managerial process by asking readers to treat all millennials the same. The tips in this chapter offer room for appreciating the diversity on your team, regardless of generation.

Summary

The Stereotype: Millennials are different from other generations when it comes to performance management and planning, reviewing, and developing performance.

The Truth: Performance management should be customized to the individual, not the generation of the individual.

What a manager should do about it: Ignore the stereotypes and embrace the individuality of your team members.

Performance Planning

1. Break goals and expectations into two categories: results and behaviors.
2. Connect an employee's goals and expectations to those of the organization.

Reviewing Performance

1. Communicate the purpose and value of the review process.
2. Establish a cadence that works for you and the employee.
3. Promote a feedback culture on your team.
4. Structure your feedback in a framework that leaves no room for misunderstanding.

Developing Performance

1. Create development goals.
2. Create formal and informal development opportunities.
3. Give employees visibility into your organization's operations.

7

Collaborative Teamwork

In this chapter we will look at stereotypes associated with teamwork and collaboration as it pertains to millennials and the other generations. First, we will meet Lorraine, the epitome of the stereotypical millennial. Then, we will look at the origin of this generalized stereotype and examine the flawed research that supports it. Finally, we will provide some key tips on creating a collaborative team while avoiding the stigma of generational stereotyping.

The Stereotype

Lorraine represents one of the most pervasive myths in the research literature. She is a millennial with an almost insatiable need to collaborate. Her ideal workplace is a synergistic swarm of cyber-connected kids. This need is fueled by the all-encompassing presence of game technology in her life, as well as her addiction to sharing personal information on the web. Since she spent her formative years highly involved with all forms of social media, she wants to continue constant interaction even in her workplace.

Before looking into the research in order to refute this myth, I will delineate some of the false conclusions that have been drawn from false assumptions:

- Since they have long operated in a world of virtual reality games, like *World of Warcraft*, the younger generations are much more adept than their elders at collaborating in worlds that transcend time, space, and language.
- Since millennials grew up in the information-sharing age, they are thought to be more vulnerable to rumor, innuendo, and suppositional content. Now that user-generated content outpaces the old-world style of expert-generated,

verifiable content, they seem to be comfortable relying on crowd-sourced information and Wikipedia references, as opposed to peer-reviewed research articles or the Encyclopedia Britannica.

- Since millennials are not content merely to watch music videos on television, they post their own videos on YouTube in hopes of achieving instant stardom—or at least the 15 minutes of fame they have been promised.

- Since millennials are completely comfortable bringing their collaborative world into the office, they welcome all manner of collaboration technologies. (Later, I will discuss the economic opportunities this myth has created for software, consultants, etc.)

- Since millennials grew up in a time in which they were highly supervised, they were often carpooled around to highly structured events, such as sports and/or cheerleading competitions. These activities supposedly instilled a sense of team spirit that they bring with them into the workplace.

- Since millennials are the most racially diverse generation in history, they obviously must respect and welcome diverse opinions. Millennials are the driving force behind gay marriage, the Black Lives Matter protests, immigration reform, and the legalization of marijuana. This respect for diversity must automatically translate into a desire to include co-workers with differing opinions, values, and perspectives.

This neatly packaged profile of "Generation Collaboration" has been shared, copied, and retweeted by businesses, writers, pop psychologists, and sometimes reputable PhDs, because it seems to make sense. In fact, these gen-experts are looking at the data through the colored lenses of unverified, and often hurtful, common knowledge.

The Error in Stereotypes

Managers are inundated with blog posts, articles, podcasts, research studies, and books that identify and support the generational stereotype; even more damaging is the research presented that supposedly proves it. As we've seen in previous chapters, these studies are often unreliable, misleading, poorly analyzed, or simply wrong. Why is this happening?

Some writers might be using the stereotypes to sell product (subtly or not). Cisco (2015), for example, has published several corporate blog posts that support the idea that millennials need to collaborate. They may quote a study or cite a panel discussion, but these articles come with a barely concealed agenda. Cisco sells online collaboration tools; it has a vested interest in persuading corporate America that we are surrounded by a generation of tech-savvy, connected employees who are ready and willing to collaborate online.

Then there are the articles that may present well-researched data but in a massaged form, twisted and stretched to make a point. For example, an article posted on a search engine homepage cited a comprehensive qualitative and quantitative study that IBM published in 2014. The article discussed how most millennials (56 percent) feel they make better decisions when a variety of people provide input. An equally high number (55 percent) felt that group consensus is important. The author (not associated with IBM) asserted that IBM's study supported his thesis that millennials are a new collaborative workforce. The article failed to mention, however, that the exact same study also found that generation X agreed with those statements at 65 percent and 61 percent, respectively. That is higher than the millennials' percentages. Digging deeper, the IBM study presents significant evidence that millennials are no more a collaborative generation than the other generations.

When asked what it takes to engage employees at work, fewer than 30 percent of millennial respondents selected a collaborative work environment. Generation X and baby boomers both scored slightly higher on this point. However, by and large the three generations were the same across the board.

Many authors writing in the field make invalid assumptions drawn from credible research. Numerous studies by research institutions, such as Pew Research Center and Pricewaterhouse-Coopers, have shown that millennials use social media as a primary forum for communication and information gathering. It may seem safe to assume from this data, then, that millennials also want to use these tools in the workplace. Technology, the studies argue, is a means to efficiency for millennials and keeps the generation connected. Therefore, the studies conclude, managers should use social media and other technologies to create a virtual collaborative environment in the workplace. However, a study by Kelton, published by Cornerstone OnDemand (a talent management, software-as-a-service company), revealed that 60 percent of millennials would prefer to collaborate in person versus online in the workplace. Also, the IBM study referred to earlier shows that millennials' penchant for social media in their personal life does not necessarily translate to a professional preference. More than any other generation, millennials keep their personal and professional social interactions separate (only 7 percent of baby boomers do, as compared with 27 percent of millennials). The meaning is clear: collaboration at home does not translate to collaboration at work.

So now let's examine the diversity issue. Do millennials truly value diversity? It is true that American millennials are the most diverse generation in history. In 2014, Pew Research Center found that 43 percent of millennials in America were nonwhite. Being the most diverse generation, though, does not justify the sweeping generalization that they are, therefore, the generation that values diversity most. The IBM Institute for

Business Value Millennial Survey 2014 found that millennials did not prioritize diversity more or less than any other generation. When asked about top career goals, working with a diverse group of people was rated as a top priority by only about 20 percent of millennials, similar to all other generations.

What becomes clear when researching a broad spectrum of studies is that factors other than generation have significantly more impact on valuing diversity—factors such as gender, nationality, and socioeconomic status. The most comprehensive metastudies on generational issues were conducted by Universum (an employer-branding firm), in partnership with the INSEAD Emerging Markets Institute and The HEAD foundation (2014a–f). The researchers surveyed more than 16,000 millennials globally and found that 28 percent in the United States highly valued having managers and fellow employees from diverse backgrounds. However, only 14 percent of millennials in Canada felt the same. The same study also found a strong gender variance around this issue as well. Millennial women were 12 percent more likely than men to cite equality and diversity as an important aspect of employer culture.

Evidence shows that millennials could even be *less* collaborative than other generations. Pew Research Center (2010b) evaluated trends in social trust over time. Less social trust could translate to less desire to collaborate. In 1997, the percentage of people over 30 who believed the statement, "Most people can be trusted," was at an all-time high of 48 percent. These were baby boomers. The gen Xers were much more skeptical at the time, rating most people as trustworthy at only 35 percent. When surveyed in 2010, the percentage of 18–29-year-olds (millennials) who agreed with that statement was only 28 percent. According to this study, then, the generation most often stereotyped as "skeptical" (baby boomers) has the most social trust, whereas the most supposedly collaborative generation (millennials) has the least. One online article that acknowledged this finding concluded that this rise was probably due to the increase in terrorism. That is a leaping assumption.

Further evidence that millennials are, in fact, less collaborative is found in the 2015 Millennial Majority Workforce study, commissioned by Elance-o-Desk and Millennial Branding. They asked 200 managers how they perceived each generation's working style. Millennials were perceived as much less team-oriented than their generation X counterparts. Only 27 percent of hiring managers perceived millennials as being team players, as compared with 73 percent of gen Xers. Clearly the millennials with whom these respondents worked did not seem very collaborative.

However, reading this study a bit further we learn that the millennials may have been misunderstood. The same 200 managers were asked what they thought was the millennials' highest priority. Only 12 percent of managers believed that "people/team" would be a top priority for millennials. In reality, 39 percent of millennials rated "people/team" at the top! It came in second after earning potential.

Overcoming the Stereotypes

With so many surveys, studies, research, articles, blog posts, and opinions, it is understandable for any manager to feel overwhelmed with the data, confused about reality, influenced by popular opinion, and unclear on steps forward. Therefore, I encourage managers to release the need to understand the generations. Your team is made of individuals, not buckets of generations. Give no attention to the stereotypes that your employees rarely embody, and, instead, focus on the individual. It is entirely possible that you will have a team that embraces collaboration and diversity, either in person or online. It is also possible you will have a team of loners. Adding to the complexity, you will probably have people on the team who sometimes value collaboration and sometimes need to work alone, sometimes online and sometimes face-to-face. They may value diversity, or not. Perhaps they value certain kinds of diversity and not others, or value diversity for certain situations and not others. The most effective way to understand your team is to talk to your team members. There is no one-size-fits-all approach. Ask your employees questions about their working style preferences, observe their behavior when put in different situations, and respect their individuality.

Collaborative Teamwork

Having said that, it makes sense to encourage a collaborative workplace culture regardless of the generational makeup of your team. Through collaboration, new ideas emerge and creativity is fostered. Collaboration also creates personal connections among team members, which encourages loyalty and retention on the team. The following are eight managerial steps to creating a collaborative team culture:

Assess Your Own Strengths and Weaknesses. Self-awareness and self-assessment are critical tools for all leaders. Take stock of the efforts you have made (or have not made) to foster a collaborative culture on your team. You can start by examining your calendar in the past six months. How frequently did you meet with the team? How often did you celebrate team successes? How often did you hold roundtable discussions to discuss the business or how your team might encourage each other's expertise? How often did you involve your team in the work you are doing? Think of creative ways you might connect with the team more often.

Look for Opportunities to Involve Your Team in the Decision-Making Process. As the manager, you have a responsibility for the team. At the same time, involving your team in the decision-making process has many positive consequences. First, your team may offer a perspective that you had not considered. Being closer to the work offers them valuable, potential insight into your business. In addition, by giving employees visibility into the decisions you are making, you are expanding their level of understanding the business. This is also a development opportunity for them, as you are preparing them for the questions they will face in the next step of their career. It also demonstrates to the employees that you are interested in their opinion, helping them feel involved and valued.

Celebrate Collaborative Wins to Help Foster a Collaborative Culture. Discuss the value of collaboration with your team. Ask them to highlight successes or losses that emerge as a result of collaboration, and encourage team members to continue.

Rewards are also an effective way to incentivize the team. However, beware of individual rewards. Individual rewards might trigger a competitive mindset that is the antithesis of your goal. If you want to encourage collaboration, implement group rewards once the team reaches its goal. Group rewards will encourage the team members to think of the greater good and will foster cohesion.

Facilitate Collaboration in the Workplace with a Change in Environment. Think of ways in which the work environment helps or hinders collaboration. For example, does your office offer enough group workspace? Are the workspaces conducive to creative thinking and brainstorming? If working in a virtual environment, what technologies are the team members using to facilitate group work? What technologies have you considered but hesitated using?

In the IBM study on generational differences, employees of every generation identified the same obstacles when implementing new technology (two of which were the leader's lack of technological savvy and the leader's inability to envision future needs). Are you, the leader, preventing the team from leveraging collaborative tools that may benefit the whole? This is an excellent opportunity to involve the team in the decision-making process.

Build a Task Force on Your Team Dedicated to Creating a Collaboration Strategy. Another way to empower the team and increase collaboration is to create a temporary task force dedicated to creating a collaboration strategy. Think of this task force as a professional development opportunity for your potential top talent. The task force members will have an opportunity to think strategically, implement new systems that will benefit the larger team, and potentially gain visibility within the organization. Give them time to form as a team, identify roles within the task force, identify problem areas, and brainstorm solutions.

The task force can then present their solutions to the leader and, if accepted, will also be responsible for implementation. Not only does this act as on-the-job professional development, but it also facilitates buy-in for change. Employees are much more likely to embrace change if the change was their idea. The task force can act as collaboration change agents for the larger group.

Evaluate Which Stage of Team Development Your Team Is in and Act Accordingly. This last step deserves more attention. In 1965, Bruce Tuckman introduced his now very popular model for team development. The model identified four stages of small-team development: forming, storming, norming, and performing. The tactic managers decide to use to encourage collaboration in their team efforts should cycle through these steps as they move forward.

Forming. In the forming stage, the team is new or certain members of it are new. The team might also be undergoing a change in strategy or direction. This stage will be accompanied by excitement but also by confusion and frustration. Boundaries are being established now, and assumptions are being tested. At this stage, the team relies heavily on the team leader, since roles, norms, and expectations are still being established. If your team is in this phase, it is important to meet frequently and communicate regularly. This is a critical phase in establishing an expectation of collaboration.

Storming. The storming stage is characterized by conflict. This is the time when team members are competing for position or for their ideas to be heard, and collaboration may be at its lowest point in the process. This can be a particularly challenging time for team members who prefer to avoid conflict. At this stage, the leader must keep the focus continually on goals and objectives. As the leader, you coach the team on the *why*: why they are meeting, why they are a team, what is their common goal. This will help the team members identify the most effective way to function, both individually and together. Implementing team rewards and doling out accolades for collaboration will go a long way in this stage.

Norming. During the norming stage the team enters a more cohesive phase. Processes are in place and team members are able to move forward with their projects. As roles are clarified, members are functioning at a high level and are generally committed to the group's goals. As the team members begin to relate interdependently, this may be a good time to take stock of what might be hindering collaboration. A general sense of positivity develops in the norming stage; therefore, build on the growing sense of confidence.

Performing. In the final stage, the team is functioning at a high level and achieving results. The team has strong interpersonal relationships and work collaboratively in pursuing group goals. The members are motivated, so the leader is mostly hands-off, allowing the team to manage itself. Communication and trust are strong and the team actively solves problems. In this stage, the leader can work on generating new ideas, promoting development of the team members, and celebrating successes. Collaboration has been achieved, so the goal is ensuring it continues. Sustaining a team in the performing stage, over a long period of time, can be challenging, so don't lose sight of the goal!

Remember, this is not a linear path. Your team may be in the performing stage now, but then revert to the storming or norming stage when circumstances change. Take stock periodically to ensure that you are leading the team to a collaborative working state as effectively as possible.

Summary

The Stereotype: Millennials are a collaborative generation that will transform how your team operates.

The Truth: Millennials are not any more collaborative than other generations.

What a manager should do about it: Ignore the stereotypes and value the synergy created in collaborative cultures. Six steps to do so:

1. Take a moment to assess honestly your own strengths and weaknesses.

2. Look for opportunities to involve your team in the decision-making process.

3. Incentivize your team to collaborate.

4. Facilitate collaboration in the workplace with a change in environment or tools.

5. Build a task force within your team, dedicated to creating a collaboration strategy.

6. Evaluate which stage of team development your team is in, and act accordingly.

   - **Forming:** Meet frequently and communicate regularly.

   - **Storming:** Incentivize collaboration and celebrate group successes.

   - **Norming:** Ensure the team is equipped with appropriate tools and an environment that facilitates collaboration.

   - **Performing:** Your team is collaborating well, so keep doing what you're doing!

8

Recruiting

As the United States comes closer to full employment, many business leaders are becoming more aware of how critical high-performing individuals are to an organization. Companies are struggling to understand how to attract and retain top talent. Robert Reich, an award-winning professor at the University of California at Berkeley and former Secretary of Labor under President Bill Clinton, described the importance of recruiting top talent for businesses. He said,

> *Nowadays, any competitor can get access to the same information technology, the same suppliers, the same distribution channels, and often the same proprietary technology. The only unique asset that a business has for gaining a sustained competitive advantage over rivals is its workforce— the skills and dedication of its employees. There is no other sustainable competitive advantage in the modern, high-tech, global economy.*

According to the Pew Research Center, approximately 10,000 people will turn 65 years old every day for the next 19 years. This will be a tsunami of departing employees with deep institutional knowledge. As organizations struggle to cope with the vacuum left by retiring employees, they must also focus on recruiting heavily from the upcoming and incoming employee talent pool: millennials. This creates what is known as the talent gap, the void left by retiring baby boomers and not yet filled by millennials. In a quest to fill the talent gap, business leaders and human resource professionals are desperately trying to understand how to recruit millennials and what motivates them in order to retain the newest generation of talent and thus gain a competitive advantage over all the other businesses trying to do the same thing.

However, millennials are considered less loyal to their employers than other generations. Often perceived as opportunistic job-hoppers, millennials have a reputation of jumping from company to company in search of their perfect role. This perpetuates the notion that companies must recruit millennials differently. Companies are tempted to offer a specific set of perks that align to millennial values in order to recruit effectively.

They also are advised that traditional recruiting methods will no longer work. No longer reachable through typical channels, companies are advised to take advantage of video and social media in order to engage millennials. This chapter will identify the assumptions associated with recruiting and retaining millennials and the advice executives are given as a result. We will look at the research and then review best practices regardless of generation.

The Stereotype

Hubert is a typical millennial job seeker. Unsure of his future career goals, he is considering working for your company, as well as many others. He may show up at the presentation you give on campus, but he is much more interested in your website and social network. He feels strongly that the company for which he works must be socially responsible. Therefore, he is looking online to see what public service causes you support. Also, because he wants a fun working culture with colleagues who like to collaborate, he is connecting with employees on the corporate social media tool. He is more concerned with work/life balance than the 401k matching program you have highlighted on your website. If you are lucky enough to recruit Hubert you will have a short window of time to make him happy. If he does not like the job or if he feels as though he is not advancing quickly enough, he will quit, leaving your organization with training and recruitment costs. From this story three key stereotypes emerge about recruiting and retaining millennials:

- Millennials are difficult to retain.
- Companies must develop an employer brand that specifically caters to millennial values.
- Millennial job seekers are more interested in online communication from employers than face-to-face interviews.

The gen-experts who propose these stereotypes often work for marketing firms or digital strategy companies. Their insight is a sales pitch in disguise, feeding off executive fear of the ever-widening talent gap.

The Origin of the Stereotype

Millennials Are Difficult to Retain

One common complaint about millennials is their lack of loyalty to their employers. Reasons abound for this stereotype. Some common misconceptions include:

- Millennials have been handed everything on a silver platter by their overindulgent parents and expect the same gratification from their employer.
- Millennials are lazy from a lifetime of playing video games and are unprepared for the realities of hard work.
- Millennials, due to their avid use of technology, are accustomed to everything being on-demand and customized, which has led to high expectations.

Numerous articles refer to research that proves millennials have higher turnover rates than their older counterparts. The articles are not wrong. An often-cited report published by the Employee Benefits Research Institute (Copeland, 2010) reveals that turnover rates for employees age 25–34 is only three years, as compared to 10-plus years for employees age 55–64. Data such as these are used to highlight how millennials jump from job to job, whereas baby boomers traditionally stay loyal to their employer. However, further investigation into this data reveals a more complete truth. In the 1980s, the turnover rates for those two age groups were nearly the same, meaning that when the gen Xers were starting their career, they had the same turnover rates as millennials do today. Turnover dynamics for new entrants to the workforce are no different today than 30 years ago.

In addition, life stage plays an important role in this statistic. With a lifetime ahead of them, millennials have time to find their perfect role. Baby boomers on the other hand are close to retirement. The looming financial obligation of retirement makes them less willing to explore new careers while waiting for vesting retirement benefits. In addition, baby boomers have had entire careers, during which they were able to experiment in various fields in different roles. Perhaps their time to experiment in different job roles has passed. Millennials, still early in their careers, have not yet had that opportunity.

This explanation does not prevent the gen-experts from warning of the millennial generation's lack of loyalty. In 2014, when the U.S. Bureau of Labor Statistics (2014) released a report that young adults born in the early 1980s held an average of 6.2 jobs between the ages of 18 to 26, the resulting articles seemed endless. Authors suggested that this fickle generation needed the red carpet rolled out for them in order to stay put. Another statistic in the same report, however, revealed that four of those jobs were held from the ages of 18–22, typically a time for summer jobs, part-time work, and other low-income positions. The statistic of 6.2 jobs in nine years does not accurately represent millennials joining corporate America after their undergraduate studies. Once graduated from college, the millennials held an average of two jobs in the next five to six years.

Companies Must Develop an Employer Brand Catering to Millennial Values

Employers are often advised to attract millennials by offering a work environment that matches millennials' supposed values. These include work/life balance, social responsibility programs, a collaborative culture, and so forth. It is assumed by gen-experts that millennials have different motivators than those of older generations. Typically this means their employers should highlight the following:

- Meaningful work.
- Rewards and recognition for a job well done.
- Social responsibility by a company that encourages its employees' involvement.
- Flexible work/life balance options.
- A fun and collaborative work culture.
- Opportunities for advancement within the organization.

(See Chapter 5 for more information on stereotypes associated with motivation and employee engagement.) Given this list of demands, executives can be excused if they are intimidated by the high expectations of millennials. Don't be intimidated; these are simply unfair stereotypes.

A study of 16,000 millennials, conducted by Universum in partnership with the INSEAD Emerging Markets Institute and the HEAD foundation (2014 a–f), revealed that what millennials want in a job varies considerably due to a variety of other factors, such as gender, nationality, and even the age of the millennial (younger versus older millennials). In addition, an IBM Institute for Business Values (2014) study revealed little difference in the motivators for each generation. Regardless of generation, employees had similar values, similar motivators, and similar reasons for leaving a position.

Even if employer branding is important in attracting talent to an organization, do they really need a strategy specifically designed to meet supposed millennial values? What is important to individual millennials varies as widely as it does among gen Xers and baby boomers.

Millennial Job Seekers Prefer Online Communication from Employers

Millennials have long been considered "digital natives." Digital natives are those born and raised in the age of digital technology. Because they were exposed to technology at a young age, they are "natives" to the language of technology. Gen Xers and baby boomers are considered digital immigrants; they did not learn the technology as a child. They do not "speak technology" with the same ease and comfort as millennials. As a result of this stereotype, millennials are often considered more comfortable with technological communication than they are with face-to-face interactions. Numerous studies show this is not always the case.

Gen-expert advice abounds on how to reach tech-savvy millennials. Executives are told to leverage social networks, construct flashy websites, and produce professional but short videos to reach these younger candidates. Millennials are considered less interested in the "old-fashioned" tactics, such as career fairs. However, when the Universum study asked millennials about their most commonly used method of learning about a potential employer, the respondents said the employer's website (55 percent). When asked their preferred method of learning about an employer (not necessarily how they learn, but how they prefer to learn), the top two choices were employer presentations on campus and career fairs. These are face-to-face methodologies. Preferences also varied by country. Millennials in countries such as France and China were not as interested in social networks as those in other countries, for example.

Overcoming the Stereotypes

The following provides suggestions for recruiting a multigenerational talent pool. The key is to authentically and effectively communicate your company's culture and values to high-potential candidates. However, beware of defining "good fit" by generation.

Do Not Create a Recruiting Strategy Around Generational Stereotypes

Though this type of recruiting is common and may seem appealing, the risk is high. A few years ago, I met a baby boomer who had recently been hired at a small tech startup in Silicon Valley. She was thrilled by the opportunity and was tasked with building her team fairly quickly. This was a wildly innovative company, started by a tech visionary. She asked for my help in hiring millennials—and only millennials—"because we are a young, innovative organization on the cutting edge of technology. We need people who are innovative, so they will fit in with our culture." When I asked her if a millennial had started the company; she replied that, no, it was started by a baby boomer, with a lifelong career in the tech industry. So, here we have a baby boomer who hired another baby boomer with a mandate to hire only "innovative" millennials. The company and the recruiter believed the stereotype, without realizing that they, themselves, broke the mold. These two innovators were sure that innovation could not be found among their peers.

I tactfully challenged her blanket assumption that millennials are innovative: "Innovation is such a vague term. How many new ideas or original thoughts must people have before they can attach the label 'innovative' to their personality? Are all millennials innovative?" I asked. "What if you hire one who isn't? What if someone from the silent generation is the most innovative person for the job?"

She quickly backtracked: "Of course it's possible, but chances are higher that if I hire a millennial, they will think differently."

"Differently from what?" I asked. "Differently from their baby boomer team leader and the baby boomer CEO?" She laughed and said she would figure it all out in the interview process, but that she would be interviewing only millennials!

This is an example of how these false generalizations endanger true understanding. This team leader is depending on a stereotype for a crucial business decision. Even when we stereotype with positive attributes, we are creating false images that are not necessarily reflective of the person we see in front of us. If the millennial she eventually hires turns out to be not particularly innovative, he or she will be the victim of unfair expectations. These expectations eventually will create problems at performance review time and will result in expensive employee turnover.

In addition, creating a recruiting strategy around generational stereotypes can be a morale-killer for current employees of other generations. What message is being sent to the gen-X employees who might work at that Silicon Valley tech start-up? If millennials are the innovative group, does that mean gen Xers are not? Would not a less harmful goal be to create a recruiting strategy for "innovative candidates" rather than "millennial candidates"?

Be Authentic about Your Employer Brand

Rather than trying to anticipate and advertise what millennials (or any candidates) might want in a potential employer, be authentic in what your organization has to offer. Misleading recruitment campaigns will lead to disappointed new hires who jump ship once they are on board and see your true colors. This hiring error will be costly in recruitment and training expenses. Instead, find your most engaged employees and ask them why they love coming to work. Let those "brand ambassadors" tell potential new hires why your organization is a great place to work. Authenticity resonates with all generations.

The Universum study mentioned earlier asked millennials which sources of information influence them most when considering potential employers. The top two responses were other students and other contacts who had worked at the company. Authenticity is key, as candidates will be asking your employees for opinions about your company.

Authenticity applies to all recruiting collateral material as well. For example, avoid using stock photos. They feel less personal than authentic photographs. High-production videos may paint a nice picture, but less doctored videos also can tell a powerful story. Don't be afraid to reveal a few flaws as well. Doing so can build trust.

Use Multiple Communication Channels to Reach Potential Candidates

Employers have numerous available communication channels. These include recruiting events, such as career fairs and college campuses presentations; digital communication via the website and social networks; and word-of-mouth through external and internal referrals, to name just a few. Leverage all these avenues to ensure you are reaching interested candidates.

Also, think about how you might get creative when reaching potential candidates. For example, over a decade ago, Google posted a billboard in the heart of Silicon Valley with a complex mathematical equation. Those who took the time to answer the equation were led to a recruiting website asking for the "best engineers in the world." This unique and powerful communication channel was created to draw the right kind of candidate to Google's application process. How might your team create a similar strategy for your organization?

Summary

The Stereotype: Millennials are different and need to be recruited differently from other generations.

The Truth: Your candidate pool is made up of a diverse set of potential candidates, regardless of generation.

What should a manager do about it? Ignore the stereotypes and build a recruitment strategy that targets the right fit.

1. Do not create a recruitment strategy around generational stereotypes.
2. Be authentic about your employer brand.
3. Leverage multiple communication channels for reaching your potential candidates.

9

Technology

No generalization is more pervasive than the millennials' use and overuse of, desire for, comfort with, and connection to, technology. This section would be remiss if it did not discuss millennials' relationship with technology. This chapter will identify assumptions associated with millennials and their use of technology, as well as identify common advice given on how to manage them. We'll look at the research and then review best practices that avoid generation stereotypes.

The Stereotypes

Alison is a millennial techno-guru. She believes that technology is an asset to the workplace and society as a whole. Considered an early adopter, Alison always has the latest gadget and downloads the newest apps. She views Apple as a religion and the iPhone as her temple. Unable to step away from her gadgets, she consistently uses social media while at work. She is unable to imagine a world in which she would not have her phone in her hand or on the desk in front of her. She is also full of ideas about how the company can adopt new technologies to improve work processes. Furthermore, if the company is slow to adopt new technologies, she will think less of the organization and consider moving on.

The following are three key stereotypes about millennials and technology:

1. Millennials view technology more positively than any other generation.
2. Millennials are more comfortable adopting new technologies.
3. Millennials are always connected and prefer to interact via technology, rather than face-to-face.

These three assumptions arise from the belief that millennials are digital natives, those born and reared in the digital age. In the next section, we will look at each assumption and the research that supports or fails to support it. Finally, we will review how these stereotypes might mislead managers trying to optimize technological efficiency.

The Origins of the Stereotype

Millennials View Technology More Positively

Because millennials were reared in the digital era, they are described as techno-beings that crave and consume technology at a rate never seen before. Older generations, on the other hand, are often viewed as techno-illiterates who avoid technology and may even fear it.

These hyperbolic descriptions may sell books and magazines, but the truth is much less dichotomized. In 2010b, Pew Research Center released a study describing attitudes about technology across four generations. Every generation responded that technology makes life easier rather than more complicated. The report concludes that, in general, the age group differences on these tech-related questions were relatively modest. In addition, a study conducted by the IBM Institute for Business Value in 2015 concluded that employees of every generation have embraced the technological revolution.

A 2012 academic study in the *Journal of Leadership and Organizational Studies* found similar results (Lester, Standifer, Schultz, and Windsor, 2012). The researchers surveyed employees ranging in age from 17 to 65 in a Midwestern organization. The goal was to identify actual versus perceived generational differences in the workplace. The study found that, even though the perception was that older generations were more resistant to technology, the three generations did not express significant differences in attitudes.

Defining levels of technology use across generations can be challenging. In their effort to understand it, the Pew Research Center asked the following types of questions in their survey:

- Do you have a profile on a social networking site?
- Do you sleep with your cell phone?
- Do you use the Internet or send and receive email, at least occasionally?

Although interesting, these behaviors do not necessarily translate to the levels of technology used in the workplace. Personal and professional uses of technology are distinct. A 2013 study by Kelton, published by Cornerstone OnDemand, a talent management software provider, asked specific questions about technology use at work. It surveyed 1,000 respondents from all generations, asking how many applications the employee used for work purposes during a typical week. All three generations used applications at about the same rate. If anything, generation X results were a bit higher than millennials.

The term *technology use* is broad and encompasses a plethora of activities. Suggesting that millennials view technology more positively than other generations is a gross exaggeration and could conceivably be considered an insult to gen Xers and baby boomers, who, after all, were the ones who invented computers and the Internet in the first place.

Millennials Are More Comfortable Adopting New Technologies

Millennials are perceived as change experts. Because they have grown up in a fast-paced society, it is easy to believe that they process change at a speed not previously experienced. Therefore, they may be perceived as experts in adopting new technologies. This is often highlighted with anecdotes about the short life cycle of any given iPhone model. However, if all generations have similar attitudes about technology, as previously discussed, shouldn't they be equally comfortable adopting new technologies? This is, in fact, often the case. The Pew Research Center (2010b) studied changes in technology behaviors over time. They found that in 2005, Internet use was higher for millennials than it was for baby boomers. In 2010, Internet use was higher for millennials again. However, in comparing rates of change, both generations adopted new technology at about the same rate.

Some studies seem to indicate that technology adoption might even be lower for millennials than found in previous studies. In 2013, Cornerstone OnDemand asked their participants about "technology overload," the point at which one is overwhelmed by the problems and possibly even the advantages about life in the tech lane. They found that millennials were more likely to have experienced technology overload than older generations by a rate of almost double! One could argue that the technology overload they experienced might make millennials more reluctant to adopt new technologies. The same study asked about application use for business and found that adoption was higher for generation X than for millennials. When asked how many applications, if any, the study sample used for work purposes during a typical work week, millennials were more likely to respond "zero," "less than one," or "one to two"; whereas gen Xers were more likely to respond "three to four" or "five or more." This result might be explained by a presumption that millennials are so technologically sophisticated that they are more selective, even blasé, about the empty promises of app developers. However, it is more likely that comfort in adopting technology depends on the individual, the technology in question, the roll-out plan for said technology, and many other possible factors. The user's generation is not the most significant factor.

One challenge that many studies address is the rate at which organizations implement or adopt new technologies. The IBM study mentioned earlier indicated that all generations embrace technology, but they are also aware of the challenges their organization faces. Participants indicated that issues such as complexity of new technology or the leaders' lack of vision are serious inhibitors for workplace technology adoption. The respondents also indicated that this fault significantly impacted the customer experience.

Millennials Are Always Connected with Technology

Millennials are often referred to as the connected generation. More and more images of young people with their eyes glued to their phones are emerging as smart devices become more popular and advertised. Social networks are a new way to bond with friends and family, in ways that did not previously exist. Because this bonding takes place online, millennials are often considered more comfortable with technological interactions than with face-to-face interactions. This stereotype is rampant and can be found in any number of articles about millennials. However, studies reveal that this is not always the case.

The Kelton study, previously cited, asked millennials how they prefer to collaborate in a work setting. Sixty percent of millennials chose in-person collaboration, whereas 40 percent chose virtual options. Another report conducted by Universum (2014c), in collaboration with INSEAD Emerging Market Institute and The HEAD foundation, asked more than 16,000 millennials their opinions on a number of work-related matters. The study found that when it comes to recruiting, the two most preferred methods of learning about a business and interacting with a potential employer were employer presentations on campus and career fairs. The third and fourth options were websites and social networks. Face-to-face methodologies were more preferred!

It is important to note that in all these studies views of technology versus face-to-face contact were split somewhere between 40 and 60 percent. Although these levels may show a slight preference one way or another, they do not indicate an overwhelming preference for either. Again, managers must discuss technology preferences with their individual employees and not base their assumptions on these or any other studies.

Overcoming the Stereotypes

The term *digital native* was originally introduced by Marc Prensky in his 2001 article entitled *Digital Natives, Digital Immigrants*. Since then, the term *digital native* has been synonymous with millennials and their comfort with technology. Having grown up in the information age, millennials were born in a digital world. They speak the language of technology fluently. Gen Xers and baby boomers are the digital immigrants, born in the analogue age who, continuing the metaphor, immigrated to the digital "new world" as adults. Compare the child who learns a second language as a toddler and grows up fluent, to an adult who later decides to learn a second language but never quite masters the accent or conjugations.

As logical as this theory may seem, the terms are simply another oversimplification of the human condition. A 2009 study by Neil Selwyn on the myths and realities of digital natives concluded that young people's use of technology is varied and often times unremarkable. Not all millennials have had the same access to technology. Millennials' abilities to access technology remains strongly associated with numerous other factors, such as the socioeconomic status, gender, and geography. The Pew Research Center conducted a study on generational differences in 2010, and asked about technology use. At the time, 75 percent of millennials had created a profile on social media whereas only 50 percent of generation X had. In presenting this data, the study refers to millennials as "digital natives." On the surface, this study may seem to be compelling evidence; however, the study also broke down social networking use among millennial demographics. Although 75 percent of all millennials had created a social profile, only 52 percent of Hispanics had. In fact, Hispanic millennials had created a social media profile at the same rate as gen Xers. In addition, 86 percent of millennials who went to college had created a profile, as compared to 59 percent who had not gone to college. Although not presented or discussed in this study, it is possible that generation X's social-media use would vary according to these types of demographics as well.

Numerous other studies show that Internet use is lower among rural millennials, as well as those from families whose parents have lower levels of education.

For managers reading articles about "how to deal with digital natives," the advice is often misleading. Along with the label of digital native come many assumptions. For example, digital natives are thought to be more socially accepting of technology use. However this is assumption is misleading. The Pew Research Center (2010b) asked its participants whether it was acceptable to use a cell phone to send or receive messages or to browse the web during a business meeting. Thirteen percent of millennials responded that both were acceptable. However, more gen Xers, 18 percent, responded that it was acceptable. Baby Boomers responded positively at the same rate as millennials: 13 percent.

What is the consequence of being a digital native? How does growing up in the information age transform one as an employee or colleague? There is not just one answer to that question. Managers must take the time to understand their employees—their preferences, their technological savvy, and their skills. The following are three tips for managing employees and technology.

Take Your Time to Select the Right Technology

It is not uncommon to be swept up in technology fads only to implement something that is not the right fit for your team. When considering new options, take the time to study the data. Checking references and experiences of other organizations that have implemented the technology is an effective way to weed through the hype. Do not rely only on the sales literature; speak to similar business teams who are using the technology and have been through the implementation process.

Involve Your Team in the Process

One of the best ways to gain support for a new technology is to involve your team in the selection process. The more ambassadors you have for the new product, the more likely you will generate excitement about the change. Listening to employees who anticipate problems with the technology will definitely be beneficial. Leaders are often coached on how to overcome their employees' resistance to change. However, seen in a different light, resistance can be beneficial. Employees who are resistant to implementing a new technology might be able to offer valuable insight into potential pitfalls that may be otherwise overlooked.

Do Not Assume Technical Prowess Based on Generation

One suggestion for managing a multigenerational workforce that I have read in numerous articles is to set up co-mentoring relationships. Co-mentoring is when the two members of the pair are both mentors and mentees. Gen-experts suggest pairing millennials with older workers so that the millennials can learn about workplace etiquette, while mentoring the older member on technology use. If this suggestion were implemented with a millennial who had little tech experience, what would the consequence be? Not assuming technical prowess based on generation may seem like an obvious one, but it is your lesson from this chapter.

Summary

The Stereotype: Millennials are digital natives who are more experienced and are more comfortable with technology than other generations.

The Truth: Technology use and comfort varies based on factors other than age.

What a manager should do about it: Ignore the stereotypes and embrace the individuality of your team members.

1. Take the time to select the right technology for you and your team.
2. Involve your employees in the process.
3. Do not assume technological prowess based on generation.

Overcoming Generational Labels

10

Roadmap to Changing Your Organization's Culture

People want to stop using generational labels. They want to drop the stereotypes. Every time I speak with someone about generational stereotypes, they agree with me. When I present the pitfalls associated with generational labels, it resonates. Our society is drawing ever closer to the tipping point on generational issues. Malcolm Gladwell describes "the tipping point" as the moment of critical mass when sociological change happens and ideas or behaviors spread like viruses (2000). I believe it is only a matter of time before the word *millennial* becomes commonly resisted. We are not at the tipping point yet, but we are getting close.

Be a Maven

In order to reach the tipping point, we need a few more mavens to pave the way. Mavens, Gladwell argued, are the people who connect us with new information. They start word-of-mouth epidemics. You might also call them change agents.

If you are interested in becoming a maven, calling attention to the perils of generational hype, this chapter will provide you with a roadmap. Change starts with you; there are ways to influence change within your organization. Everyone can have influence through action.

There are six steps toward creating awareness and changing the vocabulary at your organization:

1. Be a role model.
2. Spread the word.
3. Create a coalition of change agents.
4. Review your collateral.
5. Organize a campaign.
6. Evaluate your success.

Six Steps to Change

Step One: Be a Role Model

Don't Feed the Hype. You now have a wealth of information on the misguided nature of generational stereotypes. Do not be surprised if you start to notice even more articles, blog posts, and books on the subject. What may have gone unnoticed before might now jump out at you after reading this book. Blog posts such as How to Manage Millennials and What Millennials REALLY Want may resonate more often. Your first step is to ignore the articles. Don't click in, don't share them, and don't bother. Don't buy books on generational differences, and don't sign up for seminars that amplify generational stereotypes. The less interested we are collectively, the less motivated people will be to write about it.

Be the Change. You can make a difference by increasing communication and understanding with your colleagues. Communication begins with listening, so start listening to the people in your life. Identify times when you might be applying your own bias. Knowing what you know now, notice when you might be making assumptions about someone's intentions. Are you being unconsciously influenced by the "generational differences" machine? If you are a manager, apply the lessons in Part Two of this book to improve your leadership skills. Think of other areas of your life where these lessons might apply. Share how the changes you've made have created a difference. Become a stereotype-killing maven!

Step Two: Spread the Word

Stop Generational Stereotypes in Their Tracks. Do not be afraid to speak up when you notice generational stereotyping. Do this casually and without confrontation. Simply question whether any assumption about generational differences can be applied to such a large groups of people. Think of ways you do not fit the assumptions made of your generation, and offer examples. Think of public figures or common acquaintances that defy the mold, and share those stories. You will find that most people agree fairly quickly when it is brought to their attention.

I have found it powerful to compare generational stereotyping to other instances of stereotyping. For example, in the introduction of this book I explained an activity I use when speaking with groups on generational issues. I ask for people to identify their perceptions of each generation. Once the perceptions have been gathered and displayed prominently on a flipchart, I replace the generational labels with racial ones. What happens to a generational assumption when we filter it through a race lens or a nationality lens? For example, replace the word millennial with Hispanic in the following sentences:

- Millennials are entitled.
- Millennials want to save the world.
- Millennials are lazy.
- Millennials are innovative.

It should be immediately obvious how silly these sentences really are.

Engage in Conversation.   Looking for an icebreaker? Want to start a passionate conversation at a dinner party? Ask the people in your life what they think about generational stereotypes! You don't need to be an expert to have an opinion on generations. Most people have something to say, so ask them what they think. The reason generational stereotypes continue to prevail is because not many people challenge the concept. Apply what you've learned in this book to have knowledgeable conversations about the dangers of generational labels.

Step Three: Create a Coalition of Change Agents

Find Influential Allies. Creating widespread change at an organization can be challenging. Depending on the size, some companies will be harder to change than others. At a small organization, your advocacy might be enough to transform the entire team. Those working at larger organizations have their work cut out for them.

First, create a coalition of "change agents." Once you've finished reading this book, pass it to a colleague! Find influential employees in your organization who can join you in the charge. Remember that influence does not necessarily equate with authority. Influence is a product of the network you have, the credibility you hold, and how you inspire those around you. Steer clear of negative-minded or selfish individuals who might muddle your message.

Start with Those Most Affected. Think of the people or teams in your organization who are perhaps most affected by generational stereotypes. Do you have young millennials on your team? Stereotypes apply to all generations, but millennials bear the brunt of the hype. Ask them how they are affected and if they would like to see change. Does your team have a college graduate hiring program? Speak with the recruiters or the managers of the new hires. Does your organization have an aging workforce? Ask soon-to-be retired workers how generational stereotypes are affecting them. What about your human resources team? Human resources is frequently brought into these kinds of conversations: ask if they have an opinion. Think strategically about your coalition, so that you attract passionate advocates.

Create Diversity. One characteristic of a strong coalition of change agents is diversity. Proactively recruit a diverse group of people to your team. Diversity comes in many forms. As it pertains to generations, this means both older and younger employees. It means introverts and extroverts. It means upper management and individual contributors. Look for change agents in a wide variety of departments and regions in your company. The more diverse the coalition, the more widespread the influence. Greater collaboration occurs and more original ideas surface on teams with different perspectives. This will lead to constructive debate and greater thought leadership.

Step Four: Review Your Collateral

Audit Your Internal Collateral. An important part of changing the vocabulary within an organization is first finding out where it occurs. Use your coalition of change agents to identify areas in which generational stereotypes are prevalent. Ask the team to keep their ears open for groups that might be more prone to using generational labels. Identify instances where the organization uses generational labels in training, recruiting, or internal documents. Is there any mention of generations on your website? Are there particularly visible leaders or employees that discuss generational issues frequently?

It will help to get a lay of the land and catalogue changes that need to be made before taking action. This will also help set up a comprehensive change-management plan that will guide you moving forward.

Create Communications Materials. Think of how you might succinctly convey your message in a format that is easily consumed by your organization. Are there articles you can use as supporting documentation? Does your organization share PowerPoints via email or do you share messages via social media? Tailor your communication materials to the channels frequently used in the workplace.

It is also important to consider your key message. Why is there a need for change at your organization? In what ways have generational stereotypes been a problem? What assets will be most useful to you and the coalition in creating change?

Step Five: Organize a Campaign

Know Your Talk Track. The coalition should be creating opportunities to share the message. Ensure that you and the coalition know in advance what points you want to cover. What is your elevator pitch? What are the key points you hope to convey?

Ideally, you will find an audience with the leaders of the organization. Changing business vocabulary is easier when the leaders are on board. When executives at the top start speaking differently, there is a trickle-down effect. A small effort on their part can go a long way. If leaders share in a town hall meeting or public presentation that they do not condone generational stereotypes, your movement will gain credibility.

Partner with Internal Groups. Find strategic partnerships within the organization that will care about your message. Does your company have any internal communities or networks, such as a young professional's network or a woman's leadership program? These internal communities are great ways get support and to spread your message. These communities typically have regular meetings or guest speakers. Establish partnerships with groups that will help in your campaign. You might even recruit more members to the coalition!

Make Training Available. Once your campaign has built momentum, consider making training available to certain teams or groups. Share your personal experiences and those of others, as well as what you have learned by reading this book. Asking others to share their experiences helps build trust among members of a team through mutual understanding and a respect for differences. Training around differences (or lack thereof) among generations could go a long way toward creating more understanding on a team.

Evaluate Your Success

Conduct a Pre- and Post-assessment. Consider conducting a simple pre- and post-assessment to discover whether your efforts have led to positive change. The reassessment could be as simple as a series of interviews with various coalition members who may or may not have experienced the consequences of generational stereotyping. You could send out an online survey using a free web tool, or keep it simple by collecting anecdotes in your day-to-day conversations about how generational stereotypes negatively impact the team. This pre-assessment will be a useful tool in building a case for change.

Once you have executed some of the plan, evaluate whether a change has been made. Again this can be done through interviews, focus groups, or surveys. Ask open-ended questions to understand how people feel about the change. Has there been a shift in culture as a result of the awareness your coalition created? If possible, investigate what business results have been impacted by this change. For more information, read the Oracle case study in Chapter 11 as an example of how to measure the business impact of soft skill changes.

Celebrate Successes. Finally, in any change initiative, celebrating success is a crucial tool in sustaining change. Celebrating success highlights the value in the work you have been doing. This can boost morale for you and the coalition. It also validates your efforts and unifies the team around a positive outcome.

Celebrating success also encourages a winning mindset. You are communicating to others that you have succeeded, and change has occurred. It highlights the value of the work you are doing and gives visibility to your efforts. It will help in attracting even more interest in the work you are doing.

Summary

If you are passionate about eliminating harmful generational labels at your organization, this six-step roadmap is a clear path to creating change:

1. Be a role model.
   - Don't feed the hype machine.
   - Be the change.
2. Spread the word.
   - Stop generational stereotypes in their tracks.
   - Engage in conversation.
3. Create a coalition of change agents.
   - Find influential allies.
   - Start with those most affected.
   - Create diversity.
4. Review your collateral.
   - Audit your internal collateral.
   - Create communication assets.
5. Organize a campaign.
   - Know your talk track.
   - Partner with internal groups.
   - Make training available.
6. Evaluate your success.
   - Conduct a pre- and post-assessment.
   - Celebrate successes.

11

Case Study 1

The following chapter is a case study documenting how Oracle created measureable business results by ignoring generational stereotypes. As an organizational development consultant at Oracle, I consult with business leaders to create solutions in organizational effectiveness. In this example, I partnered with two other consultants (Kristian and Brent) to build a training program. We were asked to create a training program for millennial, recent college graduates to address generational issues. First we conducted a thorough needs analysis to understand what was really going on. We then created a training program based on the findings. Finally we conducted a full return on investment (ROI) analysis, conducted six months after the training. In the process we identified three business results created by our program, including:

1. Increased employee productivity for new hires and managers.
2. Increased intention to stay with the company.
3. Increased employee engagement and job satisfaction for new hires and managers.

Throughout this chapter, we reference both millennials and generation Y—they are the same.

Background

Oracle is a Fortune 100 technology corporation, headquartered in Redwood City, California. The company offers a comprehensive and fully integrated stack of cloud applications, platform services, and engineered systems. With over 400,000 customers—including 100 of the Fortune 100—and revenues over $38 billion, Oracle is an industry-leading company. Larry Ellison, the co-founder, executive chairman, and CTO, is one of the most well-known chief executives in the world. Oracle also has two CEOs, Mark Hurd and Safra Catz, who lead a team of more than 135,000 people in more than 80 countries.

Central to this organization's success is the product development team, led by Thomas Kurian. Kurian has been with Oracle since 1996, and has held numerous product management and development positions during this time. He currently leads a team of more than 30,000 employees, working on approximately 3,000 product development efforts. He is responsible for the development and delivery of Oracle's software product portfolio, including Oracle Database, Oracle Fusion Middleware, Enterprise Resource Planning, Customer Relationship Management, and Supply Chain Management applications.

The product development team recruits college graduates from top universities, such as Harvard, MIT, and Stanford. Product development will hire somewhere between 100 and 200 college graduates every year. In 2011, they initiated what is now called the Oracle College Hire (OCH) program. This is an initiative to engage new college graduates for the headquarters office. The goals of the program were threefold:

1. Get new college hires quickly acclimated and productive on new and innovative work.
2. Provide meaningful events that engage new college hires and contribute to their retention.
3. Get college hires excited about Oracle so that they will act as ambassadors of Oracle to their alma mater.

The program consisted of three components: career development, speaker series, and social activities. The career development component included training to enable the new hires to quickly advance in their careers with Oracle. The speaker series invited executives and guests to speak to them about the company, industry trends, and so forth. Finally, the social activities segment encouraged a sense of community and commitment to Oracle. These social activities included Friday lunches and weekends in Lake Tahoe.

In June 2013, a member of the product development leadership team found it necessary to reach out to the manager of the Oracle College Hire (OCH) program with a perceived problem. The OCH program manager was named Kristian. The product development leader explained to Kristian that the new college hires were becoming a challenge for their managers. He felt that there were "generational issues" at play here. The millennials, it seemed, didn't understand the corporate culture, and, as a result, there were behavioral and communication issues. He was hoping that Kristian could develop some kind of acclimation training for the OCH program in order to teach the millennial new hires how to work more effectively as they assimilated into the corporate environment. Kristian, in turn, reached out to the organization development consulting (ODC) team for help.

The ODC team is a global group of more than 40 people within Human Resources, who support Oracle leaders in matters of organizational and employee development. The team's mission is to build organizational effectiveness by partnering with business leaders and human resource professionals as trusted advisors. Key areas of focus for the ODC team include improving collaboration, guiding teams to be more productive and effective, building talent capability and adaptability, aligning leaders and employees to current or emergent strategies, and engaging and retaining key employees.

In this particular case, Kristian, manager of the college hire program, asked for help in creating a training element that would address the intergenerational challenges the leader assumed managers were facing. I was asked to join the team for this project. Another member of the team included Brent, an ODC manager who was responsible for supporting the product development group. Brent was based in Chicago, Illinois, Kristian was based in San Francisco, California, and I was based in Sacramento, California.

The Request

We first met via conference call to discuss the request. During this hour-long conversation, Kristian explained that the college hires' managers had been complaining about the millennials for a number of reasons, including their poor work ethic, high expectations, low productivity, and a perceived lack of employee engagement. The managers had expressed concern that the millennial college hires were unaware of corporate norms. They were requesting an acclimation training program to help them understand expectations in a corporate setting.

I sensed a number of red flags: the first being the fact that the employees were described as millennials. As we've seen, the label millennial comes with a number of false assumptions. I was worried that the managers were making broad generalizations about their 174 employees based on their preconceived notions, perhaps supplemented by their direct experience with only a few who happened to fit the stereotype. The second red flag was that the managers felt the need to ask for outside help: a training program to address their employee's expectations. Managers should be able to resolve problems such as this by communicating directly to their employees. I worried that there existed a hands-off culture among the managers. The lack of communication could lead to a misunderstanding across generational lines.

Our first task was to understand the problem and define the program objectives.

We decided to meet with the business leader who had originally made the request. We wanted to gather more information about the nature of the problem before offering any solutions.

A week later we were on the phone with the executive who made the request. He shared that a number of his managers had come to him with concerns about the new hires. "Generally, they just have bad attitudes," he said. "I think the problem is that these millennials don't understand the corporate world.

They've been in college, skipping class, and partying. Now they come to corporate America, and they don't realize how much hard work is required. They show up late, don't want to take calls in the evening. It's a problem."

I asked the executive how many millennials he had on his team. He said that no millennials reported to him, but that he had heard these kinds of complaints from numerous managers. Finally, he suggested a solution. He said that if we deliver training on emotional intelligence, the problem might be solved. *Emotional intelligence*, a term coined by Daniel Goleman, is the ability to understand one's own emotions and use that information to guide thinking and behavior. Individuals with higher emotional intelligence take more control over their reactions and are better able to navigate the social environment. The executive felt the millennials exhibit low emotional intelligence; when they feel bored or frustrated, their natural inclination is to give up or push back. If they had higher emotional intelligence, he argued, the millennials would be better able to self-manage. This would result in higher productivity for the new hires and less difficulty for their managers.

After the call, Brent, Kristian, and I reconvened. Kristian asked if we had any prepackaged training offerings around emotional intelligence. I pushed back, "I'm not sure that training on emotional intelligence is the answer here." The leader we had spoken with did not have any new hires on his team; he had been repeating hearsay. Knowing how millennials are often perceived, I argued that this might be a case of miscommunication. Rather than make assumptions about the 174 new hires, I suggested we conduct a thorough needs assessment. "Let's really get to know the employees and manager on the team. Let's send out a survey asking for their perspective and then hold a few focus groups to follow up. We might learn that the problem isn't what they think it is." Brent and Kristian agreed.

Needs Assessment

For our needs assessment, we decided to collect both qualitative and quantitative data from both the managers and the new hire employees. Kristian discovered that the 174 college hires were distributed between 143 managers. We created one survey for the new hires and another for the managers.

Manager Survey

Our goal with the manager survey was to touch upon the following themes:

- What concerns did managers have about their millennial new hires?
- Was there intergenerational conflict?
- How did the managers perceive the new hires?
- Did the managers have high job satisfaction?

In July 2013, the following survey was released to the managers using an Oracle tool called QuickSurvey. We kept the survey short, anticipating that the response rate might be low. The survey contains numerous reference to generation Y (a synonym for millennial).

Manager Survey.

Introduction

In support of the product development Oracle College Hire (OCH) program, we created this survey for managers of new college hire employees to help us understand how well new hires are acclimating to Oracle's corporate environment. We will aggregate the results and use the data to design OCH's College Hire Acclimation training, ultimately getting your new college hires more productive, faster! The survey is anonymous, so feel free to be as open as you can. Thank you for your participation!

Overview of Themes

- Concerns managers have regarding new hire acclimation to corporate environment.
- Incidents (occurrence of) intergenerational conflict.
- Manager's perception of new hires (Generation Y).
- Manager's job satisfaction.

Questions

1. I have personally observed/experienced difficulties with new college hires acclimating to the corporate environment.
   a. Strongly Agree.
   b. Agree.
   c. Neither Agree nor Disagree.
   d. Disagree.
   e. Strongly Disagree.
2. Some of these difficulties include

   _____

   (fill in the blank). If not applicable, type N/A.
3. I have personally experienced conflict with new college hires that may be a result of generational differences.
   a. Strongly Agree.
   b. Agree.
   c. Neither Agree nor Disagree.
   d. Disagree.
   e. Strongly Disagree.

4. Conflict with new college hires that may be a result of generational differences occurs:

   a. Very Often.

   b. Regularly.

   c. Sometimes

   d. Once or Twice.

   e. Never.

5. Examples of these types of conflict include

   _____

   (fill in the blank).

       If not applicable, type N/A.

6. In your opinion, please rate how often the aforementioned conflict with new college hires affects your productivity.

   a. Never.

   b. Once or Twice.

   c. Sometimes.

   d. Regularly.

   e. Very Often.

7. In your opinion, please rate how often the aforementioned conflict with new college hires affects *their* productivity.

   a. Never.

   b. Once or Twice.

   c. Sometimes.

   d. Regularly.

   e. Very Often.

8. I believe there are inherent differences between generations, specifically Generation Y (born between 1980 and 2000) and older generations.

   a. Strongly Agree.

   b. Agree.

   c. Neither Agree nor Disagree.

d. Disagree.

e. Strongly Disagree.

9. Please describe your perception of Generation Y employees (specifically college new hires at Oracle).

_____

Fill in the blank.

10. I enjoy the work that I do.

a. Strongly Agree.

b. Agree.

c. Neither Agree nor Disagree.

d. Disagree.

e. Strongly Disagree.

11. I enjoy working with new college hires.

a. Strongly Agree.

b. Agree.

c. Neither Agree nor Disagree.

d. Disagree.

e. Strongly Disagree.

12. Why or why not?

_____

Fill in the blank.

Employee Survey

Our goal with the new hire survey was to touch upon the following themes:

- What challenges were the new hires experiencing?
- How frequently were the managers and new hires discussing these challenges?
- How did the new hire employees perceive the managers?
- Did the employees have high job satisfaction?

In July 2013, the following paper survey was released to the new hires in person.

Employee Survey.

Introduction

In support of the Product Development Oracle College Hire (OCH) program, Kristian, Brent, and I created this survey for new college hire employees to help us understand how well you are acclimating to Oracle's corporate environment. We will aggregate the results and use the data to design OCH's College Hire Acclimation training, ultimately getting you more productive, faster! The survey is anonymous, so feel free to be as open as you can. Thank you for your participation!

Overview of Themes

- Frequency of dialogue with managers regarding acclimation (to compare to postprogram application focus group).
- How participants are acclimating to corporate environment.
- Participant's job satisfaction.
- Participant's perception of managers (baby boomers and generation X).

Questions

1. I have personally observed/experienced conflict with Oracle managers that may be a result of generational differences.
   a. Strongly Agree.
   b. Agree.
   c. Neither Agree nor Disagree.
   d. Disagree.
   e. Strongly Disagree.

2. Conflict with Oracle managers that may be a result of generational differences occur
   a. Never.
   b. Once or Twice.
   c. Sometimes.
   d. Regularly.
   e. Very Often.

3. Examples of these types of conflict include
   _____

   (fill in the blank). If not applicable, type N/A.

4. In your opinion, please rate how often the aforementioned conflict with Oracle managers affects your productivity.
   a. Never.
   b. Once or Twice.
   c. Sometimes.
   d. Regularly.
   e. Very Often.

5. I engage in open dialogue with my manager about conflict that may be a result of generational differences.
   a. Never.
   b. Once or Twice.
   c. Sometimes.
   d. Regularly.
   e. Very Often.

6. I believe there are inherent differences between generations, specifically Generation Y (born between 1980 and 2000) and older generations.
   a. Strongly Agree.
   b. Agree.
   c. Neither Agree nor Disagree.
   d. Disagree.
   e. Strongly Disagree.

7. Please describe your perception of older generation employees (as they compare to Generation Y employees).

_____

Fill in the blank.

8. I enjoy the work that I do.
   a. Strongly Agree.
   b. Agree.
   c. Neither Agree nor Disagree.
   d. Disagree.
   e. Strongly Disagree.

9. I enjoy working with managers of older generations.
   a. Strongly Agree.
   b. Agree.
   c. Neither Agree nor Disagree.
   d. Disagree.
   e. Strongly Disagree.

10. Why or why not?

_____

Fill in the blank.

11. I find it difficult to acclimate to the corporate environment.
    a. Strongly Agree.
    b. Agree.
    c. Neither Agree nor Disagree.
    d. Disagree.
    e. Strongly Disagree.

12. Why or why not?

_____

Fill in the blank.

Survey Results

We sent the survey via email to managers first. The email with the survey link was sent to all 143 managers with employees in the OCH program. We gave them two weeks to respond and sent one reminder email. The survey was open from July 9 to July 18, 2013. Out of the 143 managers, 44 responded, giving us a response rate of 30 percent. Hoping for more respondents in the new hire population, we decided to use paper evaluations for the new hires. One of their social outings was scheduled for the end of July, so we distributed the survey during this trip.

Out of the 174 new hires, 54 responded for a response rate of 31 percent. By the end of July we had all of the survey responses and were reviewing the results. Our focus groups were scheduled for mid-August, and we wanted to complete a full review of the results in preparation for the meetings. We anticipated that the survey results would provide insight into how we might design the focus groups. We wanted to use the qualitative data from the focus groups to more fully understand the quantitative data we had gathered from the surveys.

Results

From the survey, four themes emerged. These were:

1. New hires and managers report little trouble acclimating.
2. Hardly any intergenerational conflict was reported.
3. Few differences were perceived across generations.
4. New hires and managers enjoyed their job and enjoyed working together.

New Hires and Managers Report Little Trouble Acclimating

The survey results surprised everyone. We immediately realized that training on emotional intelligence would not address whatever challenges existed.

The first question in the survey revealed unexpected results. When managers were asked if they had personally observed or experienced difficulty for the new hires in acclimating to the corporate environment, only 16 percent either Agreed or Strongly Agreed. A whopping 73 percent of managers Disagreed or Strongly Disagreed, whereas 11 percent had no opinion. Our immediate impression was that our services were not needed. If only 15 percent of managers felt there was a problem acclimating then did we really need to design an acclimation training program?

When asked in Question 2 to describe any acclimation difficulties, most managers wrote N/A. Of the few that did respond, most difficulties had to do with new hires overcoming logistical challenges associated with the new role. Only two comments reflected the view that new hires had an inherent attitude problem or behavioral deficiency. These were:

- "Adjusting to a results-oriented mentality; it's not how hard one works as much as whether the product is completed and delivered."
- "Working within a team rather than as an individual seems to be a challenge for grads from top universities. … This has led in some cases to a college hire remaining 'stuck' on an issue and not wanting to ask a teammate for help despite lots of encouragement to do so."

When asked if they personally had difficulty acclimating to the corporate environment, only 11 percent Agreed or Strongly Agreed. Of the new hires, 57 percent Disagreed or Strongly

Disagreed, whereas 31 percent Neither Agreed nor Disagreed. When asked to expand on this, most comments were positive, reflecting reasons why they had no problem acclimating. Of those who claimed having some difficulty, answers included:

- "Need more time to get used to it."
- "Too much hierarchy compared to the school environment ... the rest is fine."
- "9-to-5 is an unusual schedule for someone who skips classes."
- "As in every new place I have to get adapted to the work culture, the people, and place itself. I do make consistent progress day to day."

Hardly Any Intergenerational Conflict Reported

Both groups also reported little intergenerational conflict. When managers were asked if they had personally experienced conflict that might be attributed to generational differences, 0 respondents said Agree or Strongly Agree, 7 percent said Neither Agree nor Disagree, whereas 93 percent Disagreed or Strongly Disagreed. When asked how often conflict that may be a result of intergenerational differences occurs, 87 percent said Never, 11 percent said Once or Twice, and only 2 percent said Sometimes. When asked to describe the conflict, all but three managers wrote N/A. The three who did respond wrote the following:

1. "Occasionally one will mumble about four-day workweeks and six-hour workdays, yet others focus on their jobs and learning."
2. "The biggest difficulty is in helping them adjust from their consumer-oriented mindset to one that focuses on the enterprise."

3. "We have sometimes seen lower self-motivation/drive that seems to stem from not really feeling like they need to try hard to make a good impression with the team—this isn't really a conflict as such but I would consider it a generational difference."

When asked how often any intergenerational conflict affects their own productivity, more than 90 percent of managers responded Never. Meanwhile, when new hires were asked how often intergenerational conflict affected their productivity, 87 percent said Never.

New hire claimed slightly higher instances of intergenerational conflict. Only 15 percent of college hires Agreed that they had personally observed or experienced conflict as a result of generational differences. Zero college hires Strongly Agreed. When asked how often the conflict occurs, 50 percent responded Never, 22 percent responded Once or Twice, and 28 percent responded Sometimes. In providing detailed comments about the conflict, the following responses were provided by college hires:

- "Different attitudes towards work."
- "My manager gives me unrealistic deadlines."
- "I have seen conflicts that result from employees who have been at Oracle for a while feeling that the company paid more attention to new hires. Nothing major, however."
- "Time balance."
- "Working hours."

New hires also felt that intergenerational conflict did not strongly affect their productivity. When asked how often the conflict affects their productivity, 65 percent said Never, 9 percent said Once or Twice, 22 percent said Sometimes, 2 percent said Regularly, and 2 percent said Very Often.

In addition, new hires indicated that they do not engage in open dialogue with their managers about conflict that may result from generational differences. Two percent said they do so Regularly, 20 percent said they do so Sometimes, 7 percent said Once or Twice, and 70 percent said Never.

Few Differences Perceived Across Generations

Interestingly, managers were less likely to believe there were inherent differences between generation Y and older generations than did the new hire employees. When asked if there were differences, only 2 percent of managers Strongly Agreed, 11 percent Agreed, 41 percent Neither Agreed nor Disagreed, 30 percent Disagreed, and 16 percent Strongly Disagreed. When asked to describe their perception of the generation Y employees, the managers overwhelmingly wrote positive comments. These included:

- "They are very eager to learn, quick to adapt and always looking forward to taking challenging tasks."
- "They are fine."
- "The most significant thing I have noticed is that the Gen Y new college hires are not at all afraid to take chances."
- "They are extremely smart and bring in a new level of energy and a fresh perspective."

Those who had a negative perception of the generation Y employees shared comments such as:

- "Those who work succeed. This has always been true. Some feel 'entitled' yet others are grateful and hard working."
- "New college grads require hand-holding for a few months before they become productive."

- "From a professional perspective, broader knowledge of technology but in general lacking the depth, so it takes a while to get them to learn and become productive."
- "We have sometimes seen lower self-motivation/drive."

New hires were more likely to believe there are inherent differences between generation Y and older generations than their managers. Of the respondents 7 percent Strongly Agreed, 39 percent Agreed, 39 percent Neither Agreed nor Disagreed, 11 percent Disagreed, and 4 percent Strongly Disagreed. In addition, when asked to provide details about the differences, the comments were evenly distributed between positive perceptions, negative perceptions, and a feeling that generations are no different from each other. The negative comments included:

- "I feel that older generation employees are a little more difficult to be convinced for changes."
- "We work a lot faster than older generations."
- "They are more serious, less interactive."
- "They think millennials are entitled."

Positive comments from the new hires included:

- "Work hard, detail oriented."
- "They have much experience. I can learn a lot from them. Also they are open minded of the new knowledge and our opinions."
- "Professional, on time, organized."
- "They are more thorough with their concepts."

Many also offered that there were no discernable differences between the generations:

- "Nothing much."
- "I don't think older generations inherently think differently."

- "It depends on the people's personality. It's hard to say that it's because they're old."
- "Depends on the person."

Finally, there were also many comments about how older generations were family oriented. The college new hires indicated that since their managers had families, their family responsibilities increased. Numerous comments indicated that their college new-hire colleagues, however, were more available for after-hour socializing.

New Hires and Managers Enjoy Their Jobs and Enjoy Working Together

Finally, both managers and new hires indicated that they enjoyed their jobs and enjoyed working with one another as well. When asked if they enjoyed the work they do, out of 44 managers, only one reported that they Disagreed. Zero reported that they Strongly Disagreed. When asked if they enjoyed working with the college new hires, zero reported Disagree or Strongly Disagree. Only one person reported that they Neither Agreed nor Disagreed. The overwhelming majority indicated that they enjoyed working with the college new hires. When asked to provide further detail, comments were very positive. These comments included:

- "I like their enthusiasm."
- "I have seen a great sense of passion."
- "New college hires are usually motivated and eager to learn."
- "They are willing to learn."
- "We have been able to hire very smart, very motivated developers through this program."

Only one negative comment was provided. The manager said:

- "I need to spend quite some time training on some basic skills."

New hires agreed that they enjoyed the work they were doing and enjoyed working with their managers. When asked if they enjoyed the work they were doing, only 10 percent of college hires Disagreed or Strongly Disagreed. When asked if they enjoyed working with their managers of older generations, only 8 percent Disagreed or Strongly Disagreed. Again, comments were overwhelmingly positive. These included:

- "They are supportive and patient."
- "They are nice guys."
- "It's a good learning experience."
- "They give us a lot of freedom and don't micromanage."
- "They are knowledgeable."

Some negative comments included:

- "He doesn't encourage me to learn new stuff."
- "I feel it takes too much time for them to pass on their vast knowledge."

Focus Groups

Once we had completed the analysis of the survey data, Kristian, Brent, and I met for another conference call. We were all surprised by the survey results. It was curious that we had been asked to build an acclimation training program, when the employees themselves reported little if any problems acclimating. Despite a few comments from one or two managers, there was little indication that intergenerational conflict existed. Respondents seemed to feel positive about their jobs and working with their colleagues. We felt strongly that the focus group would be a good opportunity to shed more light on the real issue.

We held four focus groups with 12 participants in each session. The first two focus groups were for managers based at Oracle headquarters who managed at least one of the college new hires. The third and fourth sessions were for the college hires. I facilitated the sessions, and Kristian and another colleague observed and took notes. We felt that two note takers would be necessary to capture all the comments because the session was not being recorded. Having two note takers also allowed me to focus on the participants and engage in active listening without being distracted. The sessions were each 90 minutes long.

Once the participants were seated, I welcomed them to the session and indicated that we would be talking about the Oracle College Hire Acclimation Survey results. "Our goal today is to get your opinions, impressions, and feedback in a number of areas related to Oracle College Hire acclimation. Your feedback is important to us." I also shared a few ground rules. These included:

- Everyone's ideas and opinions are valuable. We want to hear from each one of you.
- We ask each of you to treat today's conversation as confidential.
- When you have an example to share, please avoid using names or identifying specific people.
- We have a number of items we need to cover today, so please understand if I need to move us to another topic.

Focus Group Results

The tone of the focus groups was vastly different from the survey results. Although very few issues were notable in the survey, three main themes emerged from the manager focus groups including:

- Managers felt the generational cohorts were different.
- Managers claimed the generation Y employees did not understand the difference between social and professional networking.
- Managers reported that generation Y employees had low emotional intelligence.

Meanwhile, the new-hire focus groups also took a different tone. The themes included:

- New hires wanted more information about why their jobs mattered.
- New hires felt their managers could communicate more and better.
- New hires indicated that they were struggling to find work/life balance.

Kristian, Brent, and I used the challenges that were identified in the survey as themes for our training development.

Training Programs

Objectives

Over the next two months, Brent, Kristian, and I designed a training program to address the needs of the managers and new hires. Our first task was to identify the program objectives. These were the following:

1. Identify age-related stereotypes: This engagement began when an executive asked for help in addressing intergenerational issues between managers and generation Y new hires. Although most of the survey respondents indicated there were no generational differences, all three of us saw instances of generational stereotyping in the focus groups. Given my previous research, I also knew that all corporate professionals are bombarded with information on generational differences. I wanted to ensure that managers and new hires were not falling into the trap of believing the stereotype.

2. Facilitate trust and understanding between generational cohorts: As an organization development consultant, I take advantage of any opportunity to build trust and understanding on a team. The three of us noticed an us-versus-them mentality in both the managers and new hires during the focus groups. We felt that this divide could create an unhealthy working relationship in the future. We wanted to ensure that managers and new hires understood each other. With greater understanding comes greater trust.

3. Open new channels of communication between managers and new hires: One way to facilitate trust and understanding is to encourage higher-level communication, so we felt it important for both managers and new hires to see a comprehensive report of our needs assessment. We also wanted to create time during the training for managers and new hires to discuss the information we were giving them. Our concern was that managers would not follow up with the new hires, or that the new hires would not speak up. In addition, in the focus groups, new hires clearly identified "more and better communication" as a need from their managers.

4. Enhance new-hire understanding of Oracle and the new-hires' role in it: Oracle is a large organization with

many moving parts. New hires expressed confusion about their role in the bigger picture. Specifically, in the focus groups some said they would like to know why their jobs mattered. Therefore, we planned to explain organizational dynamics of this large organization: Oracle's ecosystem and structure, resources for learning more, and the Oracle strategy. We also wanted to review Oracle's short-term and long-term goals, as well as the full product stack (product offerings) in detail.

5. Improve new-hire self-awareness in order to address appropriate relationship building: Managers in both focus groups addressed a need for higher emotional intelligence. The managers felt that millennials did not have, what they called, "social awareness." They also felt that new hires were not clear on the difference between social and professional networking. This was manifesting in two ways: First, new hires were not comfortable with professional networking outside of their team. The new hires themselves confirmed this in their focus group. Second, managers felt that new hires had unprofessional relationships with their colleagues because they had developed close relationships with them.

6. Address concerns regarding work/life balance: Finally, new hires expressed concern that they were unable to manage a comfortable work/life balance. We wanted to define work/life balance for the new hires, identify what options they had available to them, and encourage them to discuss any challenges with their manager.

Training Session for Managers

Before training the new hires, we held a 90-minute virtual training for the managers. We felt it was important to share the new-hire training content with the managers before delivery to their employees. We had also planned a breakout hour during the new-hires training, when they would confer with their managers on what they were learning. We wanted to ensure that managers were prepared for the conversation. The following is a description of the 90-minute manager training session.

We had four objectives:

1. Discuss some of the myths of intergenerational dynamics:

    The request for training came from a leader who believed that intergenerational differences were creating problems on the teams. The survey results and focus groups revealed that many of the managers disagreed. The new hires considered generational differences to be minimal. As a result, we began the training with a conversation around generational stereotypes.

    After specifying the defining years for each generation, we asked the managers to identify stereotypes commonly associated with each generation. Because of the context in which we were discussing generational issues, we focused more time discussing millennials specifically. Managers revealed that they were often perceived as entitled, lazy, and impatient, but also energetic and tech-savvy. Many managers agreed that these traits were not always accurate in describing their team members.

    I began the conversation with a story that highlighted how generational assumptions may have been detrimental in my own work experience. As a trainer, I am often advised to incorporate technology into my training sessions in order to engage millennials. The preconceived notion is that they are tech-savvy so they will feel more engaged in learning when technology is incorporated. I asked the managers how many of them felt that I was making a safe assumption. The majority of managers raised their "virtual" hands.

I asked them if it would surprise them to learn that numerous studies show that millennials actually like learning online *less* than baby boomers. The managers were surprised. One study posited that older generations were more reflective learners and, therefore, do better in an online environment working at their own pace. Another argued that millennials were more active learners who crave collaboration and cannot get the community they crave via e-learning. Another said that online tools for learning are far behind other technologies that millennials use every day; they are, therefore, unimpressed with the graphics and frustrated with the programs.

I explained that my argument was not that older generations prefer online learning. My argument was that the people being studied in these particular research projects did not fit the stereotypical mold. It's worth considering that Oracle employees (or some Oracle employees) would not fit the mold either. If I were to create a tech-infused training program, based on the stereotype that millennials prefer online learning, I might disengage my learners unnecessarily. In the same way, if the managers make judgments about their employees based on stereotype, they might also be steered in the wrong direction. This example, it was hoped, would open the conversation.

I then reviewed other examples of contradictory research presented by various generational experts in the field. For example, author Neil Howe argues that millennials want job security and want opportunities to advance within a single organization (Howe, 2000). Authors Sujansky and Ferri-Reed of *Keeping the Millennials* argue that companies must cater to millennials or face high levels of turnover (Sujansky and Ferri-Reed, 2009). I asked what stereotype the managers had heard. There were conflicting perspectives among the managers in the room. I also asked the managers to consider how they might act differently if they believed one or the other stereotype. This example highlighted how preconceived notions might impact a manager's effectiveness.

2. Revealing the results of the survey and focus groups to managers:

   After discussing generational stereotypes broadly, we shifted the discussion toward Oracle new-hire employees specifically. In the session, I gave managers full visibility into the survey and focus group results, along with possible implications.

   First we reviewed the key themes from the new hires: work/life balance, a feeling that managers set unrealistic deadlines, understanding large organization complexity, and feeling that managers had different values.

   We told the managers how the new hires perceived them. Some keywords were *hard-working, knowledgeable, open-minded, serious, lacking creativity, experienced,* and *family oriented.* Then, how managers perceived the new hires: *smart, flexible, energetic, motivated,* and also *not motivated.*

   I asked managers to reflect on these results. Most agreed with the sentiments expressed in the survey. They were particularly interested in the key words managers used to describe the new hires, particularly the terms that contradicted terms, such as motivated and not motivated. Overall, they were able to relate their personal experience with these results.

3. Give managers insight into the employee training session:

   Finally, we reviewed the agenda and learning objectives for the training for new hires. There would be five sections to the training:

   - Intergenerational Understanding: The beginning of the training would be similar to the beginning of the manager session. The new hires would be asked about generation-based stereotypes, and would engage in conversation about perceived versus actual differences in generations. We would also reveal the survey and focus-group results to the new hires. It was important to us to give the new hires as much visibility into our research as we did the managers.

- Understanding Oracle: We then felt it was important to explain the complex dynamics involved in working for a global Fortune 100 company like Oracle. Not only did we break down the Oracle ecosystem and departments, but we also looked specifically at the work of each and how it fit in the larger Oracle strategy. We felt this would remove some of the mystery about the new hires' place at Oracle, as well as enhance their understanding about the value they add.

- Work/Life Balance: Work/life balance was a topic about which both managers and new hires expressed concern. The third section of the new-hire training would be a workshop around finding work/life balance. This involved a conversation about priorities, brainstorming how to find work/life balance, and reflection on realistic expectations.

- Building Relationships: The fourth section of the training session was self-awareness and self-management. The purpose was to review concepts of emotional intelligence, motivation, and the difference between social and professional networking.

- Transition Plan: Finally, and perhaps most powerfully, we would finalize our transition plan with the new hires. The transition plan was a booklet that each new hire received at the beginning of the training. Throughout the day, we would ask the new hire to write down notes, reflections, goals, and ideas on what they wanted to do differently (or transition) based on their learning.

4. Prepare managers for the conversation they would be having with their employees during training.

For each new hire, part of the transition plan involved having a conversation with his or her manager. We asked the managers to block time on their calendar and prepare for dialogue around what was learned. During our closing session we would ask the new hires what one area would they most like their manager to support. New hires would share this request and discuss any other insights they felt were relevant. We hoped to encourage dialogue and continued understanding through this process. The managers stated that they were looking forward to the conversation.

Training Session for New Hires

One week after the 90-minute manager training was conducted, we hosted two training sessions with two groups of new-hire employees, each lasting a day and a half. Sixteen employees attended the first session and 16 employees attended the second session for a total of 32 participants. The following is a detailed description of our training session.

Day One—8:30 a.m.–9:15 a.m.: Guidelines, Introductions, and Welcome. At 8:30 a.m., we welcomed participants to the room. After Kristian, Brent, and I introduced ourselves, we set guidelines for the session, including:

- Be present.
- Be open to other points of view.

- What is said in this room stays in this room.
- Participate and share best practices.
- Network and learn from each other.

We then asked each participant to introduce themselves by sharing their name, team, job role, how long they've been at Oracle, and an interesting tidbit about their life that they were willing to share with the group, such as a hobby or interesting fact. We used this time to break the ice and joke with the participants. We were also building trust and creating an environment of fun.

Once introductions were complete, we also played an icebreaker game. The game is a common theater improvisation warm-up called Zip Zap Zop, in which participants pass an imaginary ball to one another while shouting zip, zap, zop in succession. If a player accidentally says zip when they are supposed to say zop, or freezes in confusion, they are eliminated, and the next round begins. This game gets people on their feet, releases some tension, energizes the group, and breaks the ice.

Once the ice had been broken, we introduced participants to the agenda, learning objectives, and transition plan. The transition plan was a small booklet and was introduced as a tool for creating change and driving results. We explained that we would be referring to the transition plan many times throughout the day and they should be thinking about what they hoped to gain from the training.

Day One—9:15 a.m. –10:15 p.m.: Intergenerational Understanding. We began with a conversation around generational stereotypes. After defining the birth years for each generation, we asked the participants to identify assumptions and stereotypes commonly associated with each generation. We broke the participants up into four groups to discuss. We then reconvened as a larger group, and each subgroup presented a summary of their discussion. More so than the managers, new hires in both training sessions struggled to identify stereotypes associated with each generation.

I then told the story about how I would have been misguided if I had incorporated technology in the training based on the stereotype for millennials. I also reviewed some of the contradictory research presented by various "generational experts" in the field. I used the example of authors Johnson and Johnson of *Generations Inc.* arguing that millennials want job security and opportunities to advance within a single organization. Authors Sujansky and Ferri-Reed of *Keeping the Millennials* (2009), meanwhile, argued that companies must cater to millennials or face high levels of turnover. I asked the millennials in the room which felt the most true for them? The consensus was that the participants did not want to be placed in either box. This conversation was useful in identifying unfair stereotypes associated with generation.

Day One—10:30 a.m.–11:30 a.m.: Survey and Focus-Group Results. After a short break, we returned to reveal the results from our survey and focus groups. We presented the same results that were shared with the managers the week before. This included key themes identified by college new hires such as work/life balance, a feeling that managers set unrealistic deadlines, understanding large organization complexity, and feeling that managers had different values.

We then presented key words describing how new hires perceived their managers including hard working, knowledgeable, open-minded, serious, lacking creativity, experienced, and family oriented. Key themes from the managers' perspective were also presented, such as work/life balance, understanding large organizational complexity, adjusting to a results-oriented mentality, and professional versus social networking.

Finally we shared how managers described the new hires in the survey responses and focus groups, including key words like smart, flexible, energetic, motivated, and, also, not motivated.

The new hires were very interested in the results and were surprised to learn about the managers' perspective. After much discussion, we asked the participants to pull out their transition plan. In the section labeled "Intergenerational Understanding" we asked them to spend a few moments answering the following two questions:

1. What insights did you garner from the survey results?
2. How might you use this information when approaching your work/manager in the future?

Day One—11:45 a.m.–12:30 p.m.: Understanding Oracle. To begin the section on understanding Oracle and large organizational complexity, we asked for volunteers in a role-play demonstration. Many volunteers came to the front of the room to finish the following script:

- Person A: Hi friend! Where do you work?
- Person B: I work for Oracle!
- Person A: Oracle? What do they do?
- Person B: Excellent question! Oracle _____

Given Oracle's size, global reach, long history, and extensive product line, the answers varied from individual to individual. We used this game to highlight the many aspects of Oracle's business. We then discussed how Oracle is a database company, and a portal company, and an application company, and a cloud company, and a hardware company, and a services company, and so forth. Different employees have different perspectives.

To simplify the conversation, however, we showed the employees a video of Larry Ellison describing his vision for the company and discussing the strategy. We presented the different departments in Oracle and how they interact. We also looked specifically at their team, and their network of employees-partners. Finally, we completed this section with a repeat of the role-play previously mentioned. We asked the employees to present how they would describe Oracle now that they have more information. The presentations were greatly improved.

To finish this portion of the training, we asked the employees to return to their transition plan. In the section, titled "Understanding Oracle," we asked them to answer two questions:

1. How would you describe Oracle's business model?
2. What other aspects of Oracle's business model would you like to learn about? How might you go about it?

Day One—1:30 p.m.–2:15 p.m.: Work/life Balance. After lunch, Brent and I discussed work/life balance. In this section, we defined work/life balance as the proper prioritization of work (career and ambition) and lifestyle (health, pleasure, leisure, and family). We facilitated an extensive discussion about what work/life balance meant to them. We brainstormed ideas for creating more work/life balance, and discussed barriers to doing so. In the discussion, Brent, Kristian, and I also set the stage for realistic expectations. We discussed when an expectation might be reasonable and when it was not in the context of work life at Oracle. At the end of this section, we asked employees to return to their transition plan. In the section titled "Work/Life Balance," we asked them to answer two questions:

1. What realistic work/life balance issues need to be addressed?
2. What can you do to improve your own work/life balance?

Day One—2:30 p.m.–3:30 p.m.: Self-Awareness and Self-Management. Next we focused on self-awareness and self-regulation. We started with a quote from Richard Bach, author of *Jonathan Livingston Seagull* and *Illusions*: "Argue for your limitations and sure enough, they're yours." We asked the participants to reflect on the quote and many discussed their interpretations. This launched a discussion around self-awareness and emotional regulation. Pearl Buck once said that "You cannot make yourself feel something you do not feel, but you can make yourself do right in spite of your feelings." That is the perspective of an individual with high emotional intelligence. We asked participants to reflect on their own self-awareness and self-management.

To reiterate the lesson, we broke the group up into pairs. We asked each participant to tell their partner a story about their life. The first time they told the story, they were asked to tell it as if it was something that was out of their control—something that just accidentally happened to them: They were at the right place at the right time—or the wrong place at the wrong time—and there was nothing they could do to control the situation. They were victims of it.

We then asked the participants to tell the story again, a second time, from the perspective that they did have control: they made it happen. They were responsible and in charge; without them it wouldn't have happened. After sharing, we asked the participants what felt more authentic for them. They shared that owning the situation felt more real.

Finally, we distributed a self-assessment about dealing with unattractive but necessary tasks. The assessment scored them on their ability to self-manage and self-motivate. Participants were not asked to share their scores, but we did review some tactics for increasing one's score. These were tactics in self-leadership taken from the book *Mastering Self Leadership: Empowering Yourself for Personal Excellence* by Chris Neck and Charles Manz (2012).

The tactics included reminders and attention focusers, removing negative cues, self-observation, self-goal setting, self-reward, and practice. At the end of the conversation, we asked employees to return to their transition plan. In the section titled "Self-Awareness and Self-Management" we asked them to answer two questions:

1. How should I manage myself when I approach my manager on issues?
2. What self-leadership strategies will I use?

Day One— 3:45 p.m.–4:45 p.m.: Building Relationships. In the section on building relationships, Brent discussed the complexity of working in a large organization such as Oracle. It is made of people and networks, reporting structures, lines of dependencies, of partners, suppliers, and customers. This complexity can create ambiguity. He asked participants to reflect on their experience living with competing priorities, working with multiple bosses, influencing without authority, and building relationships. He also discussed four tools in building strong relationships:

- Trust others.
- Be trustworthy.
- Set/reset communication.
- Foster cooperation.

At the end of this section, he asked employees to return to their transition plan. In the section titled "Building Relationships" he asked them to answer two questions:

1. What might my manager be thinking or experiencing when I work with him or her?
2. How will I use the relationship-building tools we discussed?

End of Day One: Social Happy Hour. This concluded the first day of training. After a quick summary of the day, we invited all participants to a networking session. This session was an opportunity to build new friendships, meet new colleagues, and socialize. All participants opted to stay for the social hour, and lively conversations about the day's learnings ensued.

Day Two—8:30 a.m.–8:45 a.m.: Welcome and Recap. We began day two with another round of Zip Zap Zop. We also asked if any participants wanted to share reflections, insights, or questions.

Day Two—8:45 a.m.–9:45 a.m.: Communicating with Your Manager. The main purpose of the second day's training was to facilitate a conversation between the new-hire employee and the manager. We discussed the role of the manager and the value of being open and honest with them about needs and concerns. Finally, we asked participants to spend a significant amount of time working in silence on the final section of the transition plan titled "Preparing the Conversation." This section contained six questions:

1. What are your career goals?
2. What challenges do you have with work/life balance?
3. What is the most important thing you identified in this workshop that you should discuss with your manager? (What you want to achieve?)
4. What do you need to be aware of within yourself when you talk with your manager? (Any biases, triggers, preferences, expectations, etc.)
5. What might be your manager's point of view?
6. What can you do to gain commitment and get closure?

Day Two—10:00 a.m.–10:30 a.m.: Boss Tips. In preparation for the conversation with their manager, we provided the new hires with some basic tips in talking with their manager. Brent put together this list he called "Boss Tips." We discussed each of the following tips:

1. Know what you want to achieve. Before going into a meeting, figure out exactly what you want to achieve. Don't approach your boss with just a problem; approach with a solution, as well.

2. Anticipate the worst-case scenario. Once you've imagined your worst fears, feel confident that you can weather any negative scenario that arises.

3. Come prepared with evidence—disclose your biases. Be prepared to back up why your idea is a good one. Strengthen your argument with your quarterly review, market rates, written memos, and so forth. If you're vigilant about putting all the facts on the table when you're talking through an issue, and even acknowledge your own biases, you'll have real credibility.

4. Give the main point, and then fill in details if needed. By starting with the main point, your manager will be better able to process the details, which means you'll get a more useful answer and your manager won't dread a drawn-out conversation they don't have time for.

5. Clearly state what you need. Are you just giving your boss a heads-up of something she should be aware of? Or are you asking for approval for something? Seeking input? Clearly state what outcome you are hoping for so that they know precisely what you're looking for.

6. Be attuned to how much information your boss wants. Some bosses want to hear all the background and every option and why. Other bosses just want to hear the basics, and have little patience for the supporting details.

7. Keep your cool. Stay calm and keep your emotions in check. Even when you're frustrated or angry, you'll generally get a better result from your manager if you can remain calm. If your manager can count on you to be a rational, objective thought partner, you'll have far more credibility.

8. Be assertive and persistent. If you get a negative reaction at first, don't back down immediately. You should feel like you've had a fair hearing and discussion, and not been dismissed out of hand.

9. If the answer is no, ask for the reasons why. If there's no budging, ask if you can revisit the topic at a later date.

10. Think about the big picture. Your manager isn't only thinking about how things affect you but how they might impact the entire team. If you approach things from that perspective, too, you'll be able to preemptively think of solutions to concerns your manager has.

Day Two—10:30 a.m.–11:00 a.m.: Role-Play. Finally, before the new hires met with their managers, we gave each participant an opportunity to practice. We split everyone up into pairs and asked them to role-play the employee-manager conversation. Upon completion of the role-play each had the opportunity to give one another feedback.

Day Two—11:15 a.m.–12:15 p.m.: Meeting with Manager. Starting at 11:15 a.m., each employee had a phone call with his or her manager. Employees were sent to various breakout rooms for a quiet space to take the call. After the call they were asked to return to the training room.

Day Two—12:30 pm.–1:00 p.m.: Reflections and Close. In conclusion, we asked the participants to reflect on the calls. Many employees shared that they appreciated the structured opportunity to talk with their managers. They shared their goals and some success stories. We answered lingering questions and offered kudos for a job well done. To finish the session, we thanked all participants for their time and said we would be available for any further questions. We also pointed out to them our internal career-development site, as well as our learning-and-development site for further resources.

After each session, we gathered feedback from the participants. Since these were pilot sessions we wanted to use the participants as sounding boards for improvement. We conducted a focus group after each session to gather this feedback.

The focus group was also an opportunity for participants to provide candid on-the-spot feedback about the session. The feedback was as follows:

- Overall impression: Positive. Participants gave high marks and felt it was beneficial. They also had fun and felt it was engaging.
- Favorite part: The games, such as Zip Zap Zop, were a highlight. Employees also enjoyed the conversation around emotional regulation.
- Suggestions for Improvement: The employees suggested that more time could have been spent on networking, particularly the difference between building professional and social networks.
- Important note: Many of the participants said they were unfamiliar with generational labels prior to the training. Over two-thirds of participants in the class were born and reared in China or India.

Return on Investment Analysis

After the training was delivered, Brent and I opted to conduct a complete return on investment (ROI) analysis of the training.

Both Brent and I had completed a five-day certification course on ROI analysis for training programs that is offered by the ROI Institute. We decided to use the Phillips ROI methodology to analyze our effectiveness and efficiency in delivering the training. Before expanding the pilot training to all new hires in the product development team, we wanted to ensure that it was time well spent.

Methodology

This study was completed using the Phillips ROI methodology. This is the most widely accepted process to evaluate the business impact of training. To understand the ROI process it is helpful to examine the key steps involved in developing the ROI.

The first step is data collection. This includes baseline data; follow-up data is collected after a program has been conducted. A variety of postprogram data collection methods were used including focus groups, surveys, and tests. In order to complete an ROI analysis, five levels of feedback must be collected, including:

1. Reaction—how participants reacted to the program.
2. Learning—what participants learned in the program.
3. Application—how the participants applied the learning to their work.
4. Business Results—what business results ensued from the learning.
5. ROI—The return on investment of the program.

The second, and perhaps most important step in the model, focuses on the necessity of isolating the effects of training. In every organizational situation, a variety of factors influence the output measures of organizational or business impact.

Training is only one of many influences that drive a particular measure. One or more strategies must be selected to isolate the effects of the training.

The next step in the ROI model is converting data to monetary values. Output measures must be converted to dollar values so they can be compared to the cost of the program to develop the ROI. All fully-loaded costs that are related directly or indirectly to the training program are included in the ROI calculation. This includes participant salaries and benefits incurred while away from work to attend the training.

Finally, the costs and benefits come together in an equation for the ROI. Net benefits (the program benefits minus costs) are divided by the total investment in the training program. This provides an ROI formula comparable to ROI calculations for other investments that typically show the net earnings divided by the average investment. A final step lists intangible benefits that are very important but not translated into monetary values for the program benefits.

Data Collection I: Reaction

Reaction feedback was collected via focus group immediately following the sessions. A third party conducted the focus groups, while the instructors left the room.

Students' immediate end-of-class feedback on all aspects of the learning event was very positive:

- The participants felt that it was, generally, beneficial to them as new hires. They also felt that the training was fun and engaging.
- Participants stated that highlights of the program included the icebreaker and the discussion on emotional regulation.

- The participants requested further development of the section on professional and social networking.
- The instructors were rated highly, and most students said that they would recommend this program to their colleagues.

Data Collection II: Learning

Learners' mastery of the content and skills in the class was assessed by an eight-question, end-of-course test. The test was mostly multiple-choice but also included one short-answer question. All learners passed the test on the first try. The average score achieved was 76 percent.

Data Collection III: Application

To determine whether people were applying what they learned on their jobs, learners were asked to answer a follow-up questionnaire six months after finishing the learning event. The learner's managers were also asked to answer a follow-up questionnaire. A total of 16 college hires completed questionnaires reporting their post-training job performance. This is a 50 percent response rate.

The anticipated application of the training would allow participants to work more collaboratively with their manager as a result of reduced intergenerational tensions. In addition, it was important that learners leave the session with a transition plan that they would discuss with their manager. The self-reports of their ability to perform the suggested activities for their role were positive:

- One hundred percent of employees had a completed transition plan.
- Thirty-six percent reported increased collaboration with their manager as a result.

Data Collection IV: Business Results

In order to determine the actual impact on business, we held two focus groups, six months after the training. One focus group was for new hires and the second focus group was for managers. A total of 16 college hires participated in the evaluation focus groups six months post-training. Nine managers participated in separate manager-only focus groups, as well. During their focus group of the new hires, we asked the participants to estimate their improvement in four categories: job satisfaction, productivity, intention to stay with Oracle, and employee engagement. The managers were asked to make the same estimates with regard to their own improvement.

In order to isolate for the effects of the program, we asked each group to estimate the percentage of improvement that was due exclusively to the training. Finally, we asked each participant to estimate how accurate their adjustment percentage was.

Both new hires and their managers reported an increase in productivity. Intention to stay with Oracle also reportedly increased according to both college hires and their managers. Finally, college hires indicated that they had higher job satisfaction and employee engagement as a result of the program.

Two quantifiable business results—productivity and retention—were measured as part of the study:

Productivity. Upon joining any organization, new hires are considered a drain on productivity: they are drawing a salary, while consuming training and orientation expenses. Productivity costs were calculated using a new-college-hire salary. Simply, productivity loss is salary cost before an employee is operating at average capacity.

Since new college hires report to a variety of teams, performing different functions, one standard productivity measure (lines of code developed, number of bugs, etc.) was impossible.

Therefore, measures used included self- and manager-reported increases in productivity, coupled with a confidence factor in the program that caused the increase. Thus, the percentages below are the final figures of reported productivity increase adjusted by the confidence factor.

- Improvement in productivity was reported as 22 percent by the new hires and 10 percent by the college hires' managers. To be as conservative as possible, the number chosen is 10 percent.
- 10 percent of average salary and benefits × 16 college hires reporting = the monetary benefit in increased productivity.
  - Salary is the average of incoming college hires, as per Oracle HR.
  - Benefits are 24 percent of salary, as per Oracle Benefits, the internal group responsible for benefits.

Retention.   At the time of the post-training evaluation, all 32 participants were still employed by Oracle. Participant new hires were between 1 day and 5 months of employment when the program was run, and were under 1 year of employment at the time of the post-training evaluation. New-college-hire attrition has an upswing at one year of employment or greater. Given this timeline, retention for this program is measured by intent to stay.

Of the 16 (50 percent) who participated in the post-training evaluation, all claimed that this program was a contributing factor in their intention to stay. They stated that if the program had not been in place, they would have been more inclined to leave.

Savings were considered to be captured in the reduction of turnover costs: usual recruiting and training of replacements, among other costs. Industry research estimated average turnover cost for a product developer is 200–400 percent. In the interest of conservatism, we used the more conservative 200 percent in this study.

- Increase in intention to stay was reported as 23 percent by the new hires and 19 percent by the college hire's managers. The more conservative number is used: 19 percent.
- Average salary × 200 percent × 19 percent (conservative number from managers' reports) × 16 reporting participants **= the monetary benefit in increased intention to stay.**

We only counted these savings from the 16 participants who reported an increase in intention to stay. We did not generalize these results to all 32 participants in the program, in the interest of being conservative.

Increases in employee engagement and job satisfaction were not quantifiable, so these were kept separate as intangible benefits.

Data Collection V: ROI

For ROI, the monetary benefit from increased productivity was added to the monetary benefit from increased intention to stay.

Costs were estimated at a total of $97,416. This included development costs, calculated by using time spent, multiplied by the salaries and employee benefits of Brent, Kristian, and myself, equipment and printing expenses, facilities expenses, and travel costs.

Using the ROI formula of benefits over costs, the return was calculated at 795 percent.

Conclusion

This engagement is an example of how generational stereotypes can be overcome in order to create measurable business results. We did not believe the millennial stereotype found in the media, and we did not blindly accept "common knowledge" about their generation. Instead, we invested the time to get to know the employees on the team. By gathering extensive feedback from the new hires and their managers we were able to identify the particular challenges they faced. I believe that if we had implemented an "acclimation training for millennials" as per the original request, the ROI would not have been as high.

12

Case Study 2

This chapter will present a second case study, this time with a Class I railroad organization. In this example, the railroad organization studied was considering a significant investment in technology and training programs for the graduates of a management-training program. Making no assumptions about learning preferences, they conducted a survey of the targeted population. I consulted with the organization to create an extensive peer-reviewed study to analyze differences in learning style preferences by generational cohort. The results revealed that no correlation existed between learning preference and generational cohort. The organization then made a series of investments based on the findings. Generational stereotypes were once again proven wrong.

Background

The railroad industry has a long history of resiliency. At first, the railroads operated in the private sector. However, because of the public's dependence on fixed public transportation, a regulatory board was established in 1887 to oversee rates, mergers and acquisitions, and so forth. This board was called the Interstate Commerce Commission (ICC). Some have argued that, as time passed, the ICC became overly influenced by the industry interests. Many of the Commission members were, themselves, lifetime rail executives. By 1960, with over a third of the U.S. rail industry close to bankruptcy, it was time for change. In the 1970s and 1980s, a series of policy changes resulted in deregulation. One consequence of the deregulation was an increase in mergers and acquisitions. Although there were 56 class I railroads (i.e., railroads with an annual operating revenue of over $1 million) in North America in 1975, there were only seven class I railroads by 2005.

As railroad traffic diminished and mergers continued, the workforce was reduced. The workforce aged significantly, given massive layoffs and minimal recruitment. In seven years, the average age of a railroad industry employee increased by almost 10 years. The workforce was then largely stagnant until the early 2000s when baby boomers began to retire. It was at this time that railroad executives realized there was no talent pipeline to fill the gap of retiring employees. Complicating recruitment efforts was the fact that young people entering the workforce in the 2000s were aware of the railroad industry's unfortunate history, making it an unattractive career choice. Therefore, around 2010, it became necessary for the class I railroad companies to invest heavily in recruiting their next generation of employees.

This was the climate in 2013, when I began studying the industry. Significant investment was being made in recruitment, retention, and training for new hires to the specific organization that requested my help. Changes were made in recruitment programs and employee benefits packages, and customized employee training was necessary. At the time, over 30 percent of the workforce was eligible to retire. By 2019, it is projected that almost 50 percent of the workforce will be eligible for retirement. At the same time, new hires have little experience in the field.

The Request

In 2013, I was invited to speak at a railroad-industry human resources conference. Generational issues were and are hot topics, and the conference organizer had heard about the work I was doing. After presenting on the dangers of generational stereotyping, a man walked up and thanked me for my presentation. He was the manager of management development at a class I railroad organization. This individual was responsible for creating learning and development programs to retain the next generation of leaders in the industry. He had been reading about millennial learning preferences and intergenerational differences from the gen-experts. However, after hearing my presentation, he began to question the assumptions. He had been planning a significant investment in a simulation training program, but wanted validation that it was the right choice. He asked me to help him develop a plan for optimizing his management training program.

I suggested that we ignore the hype and conduct a study to understand his team and their specific needs. The purpose of my study was to understand the online learning preferences and learning styles of his team members. The goal was to identify best practices for instructional design in a multigenerational workforce.

The population for the study included employees that had graduated from his department's leadership development program. This program had been in effect since 2001, and participants included executives, managers, and new hires. Three generations were represented in the sample population, including baby boomers, generation Xers, and millennials.

In total, 765 participants were invited to participate. All participants selected for the study were sent email invitations with an embedded web address for an online survey. Participants were asked to complete a two-part survey. The first part was the Felder-Soloman Index of Learning Styles (ILS). This is a validated instrument that measures one's learning-style preferences: How do they like to learn? Are they verbal or visual learners, for example. The second part of the survey asked participants about their preferences for various web-based learning activities: What tools did they like to learn with—the twitter-verse or discussion boards?

The data collected through the online survey were analyzed to determine first whether any generational differences existed in terms of learning styles and learning activity preferences. The analysis would be useful to the learning and development team in order to determine best practices for training programs moving forward.

Specifically, the client was asking three questions:

1. To what extent do learning-style preferences vary by generation?
2. To what extent do preferences for learning technologies and learning activities vary by generation?
3. How can instructional design for web-based learning be optimized to address the learning style preferences of this generationally diverse workforce?

Needs Assessment: Survey

Some argue that measuring learning styles can be harmful as stereotyping, because we seem to be putting students in boxes, much like generational stereotypes do. The argument has been made that this can actually hinder learning progress. Richard Felder and Barbara Soloman (2004), the creators of the learning style test, acknowledge and generally agree with these critiques. However, they argue that the primary purpose of the "Index of Learning Styles" is to help trainers design effective learning programs. By understanding the learning style profile of a particular class, course designers and instructors can incorporate design elements that support a variety of learning styles. The danger lies in, then, applying those learning style traits to a broader population—meaning the results from this study are valid for these employees but do not necessarily represent all generations, or all railroad employees.

Data Collection

An email invitation, with an embedded URL to the online survey, was sent to all graduates of the learning program who were employed at the railroad organization. Upon entering the survey site, participants read an informed consent page, outlining the risks and benefits associated with the study and the safeguards in place to ensure individual anonymity and confidentiality. The information from the survey was kept strictly confidential. To participate in the survey, participants had to click a box indicating they had read the information page prior to proceeding to the survey. Participants, however, were able to opt-out and withdraw from the survey at any time throughout the survey administration process.

The survey administration window remained open for two weeks and an email reminder to participate was sent one week before the end to encourage participation and maximize the overall response rate. The survey came from an internal email, so the employees understood the request was coming from internal resources thereby increasing the likelihood of participation.

Survey Results

Generation. Of the 765 employees in the sample, 230 completed the survey, which represents a 30 percent response rate. Of the 230 respondents, 0.5 percent were traditionalists (born before 1945); nine percent were baby boomers (born between 1945–1963); 52 percent were generation X (born between 1964–1979); and 39 percent were millennials (born between 1980–2000).

Learning Style Preference.   There were four dimensions on which 230 participants were scored:

1. Active (63 percent) versus Reflective (37 percent).
2. Sensing (65 percent) versus Intuitive (35 percent).
3. Verbal (15 percent) versus Visual (85 percent).
4. Sequential (58 percent versus Global (42 percent).

Overall, the group of participants was classified as more active than reflective learners, meaning they preferred to learn by doing rather than by thinking, and more sensing than intuitive, meaning they were interested in learning about facts and practical application rather than abstract concepts and theories. The most striking dimension was the visual versus verbal dimension in which 85 percent of participants were visual rather than verbal. Finally, the sequential versus global dimension was the most balanced dimension, with a little over half the participants on the sequential side (learning things step-by-step) versus global learners who prefer to see the big picture.

The results of this study are consistent with previous research.

Learning Style Differences by Generation

The first research question for this study asked how the learning style preferences varied by generation. Overall, the results seem to indicate that learning style preferences did not vary significantly when accounting for generation, in this employee population. In fact, each generation fell within only a few data points of the averages cited in the previous studies that used the same Felder-Soloman Index of Learning Styles.

Given the extensive generational research that implies each generation learns differently, this was surprising. At least for this employee population, there was no discernable difference across generations.

Learning Activity Preferences by Generation

The second research question asked to what extent do learning activity preferences vary by generation. In the second section of the survey, participants were presented with a comprehensive, yet unexhausted, list of 22 web-based learning activities. The participants were asked to select their top-five favorite learning activities in terms of their web-based learning experiences. The 22 learning activities listed in the survey were:

1. Reviewing information in graphic format (tables, charts, and graphs).
2. Using search engines for online research.
3. Interacting with computer simulations.
4. Practicing real-world interactions in online simulations.
5. Reviewing quick reference guides such as FAQs.
6. Viewing video-recorded lectures.
7. Reading text (theories, concepts, nonfiction).
8. Designing/drawing concepts visually.
9. Presenting your findings to others.
10. Watching educational animations.
11. Engaging in live, short (one-hour) webinars.
12. Playing one-player computer games.
13. Interacting with peers in social media forums.
14. Chatting online with experts/specialists.
15. Engaging in virtual realities.
16. Using mobile apps to engage in learning via smartphone devices.
17. Playing multiplayer online games within virtual worlds.
18. Participating in multi-user online brainstorming centers.
19. Completing questionnaires and/or surveys.
20. Participating in online discussion boards.
21. Observing people online (desktop sharing).
22. Sharing snippets of info online in twitter-like communities.

Figure 12.1 presents a summary of the top-five most frequently selected learning activities and the bottom-five least-selected learning activities, for all participants, organized

	All Generations %	All Generations n	Baby Boomers %	Baby Boomers n	Generation X %	Generation X n	Millennials %	Millennials n
1 Reviewing information in graphic format (tables, charts, graphs)	58.1	133	52.4	11	54.2	65	64.8	57
2 Using search engines for online research	45.2	104	47.6	10	45.8	55	44.3	39
3 Interacting with computer simulations	44.3	102	61.9	13	49.2	59	34.1	30
4 Practicing real-world interactions in online simulations	40.6	93	28.6	6	45.0	54	37.5	33
5 Reviewing quick reference guides such as FAQs	32.6	75	42.9	9	30.8	37	33.0	29
6 Viewing video-recorded lectures	31.7	73	28.6	6	30.8	37	34.1	30
7 Reading text (theories, concepts, non-fiction)	31.4	72	47.6	10	25.0	30	36.4	32
8 Designing / drawing concepts visually	28.3	65	19.0	4	27.5	33	31.8	28
9 Presenting your findings to others	23.9	55	23.8	5	24.2	29	23.9	21
10 Watching educational animations	22.3	51	28.6	6	20.0	24	23.9	21
11 Engaging in live short (one-hour) webinars	18.3	42	19.0	4	23.3	28	11.4	10
12 Playing one-player computer games	17.8	41	9.5	2	20.0	24	17.0	15
13 Interacting with peers in social media forums	16.1	37	19.0	4	15.0	18	17.0	15
14 Chatting online with experts / specialists	14.0	32	14.3	3	13.3	16	14.8	13
15 Engaging in virtual realities	13.9	32	14.3	3	13.3	16	14.8	13
16 Using mobile apps to engage in learning via smart phone devices	13.0	30	4.8	1	15.0	18	12.5	11
17 Playing multi-player online games within virtual worlds	11.3	26	4.8	1	10.8	13	13.6	12
18 Participating in multi-user online brainstorming centers	9.1	21	4.8	1	8.3	10	11.4	10
19 Completing questionnaires and/or surveys	9.1	21	14.3	3	10.0	12	6.8	6
20 Participating in online discussion boards	8.3	19	9.5	2	8.3	10	8.0	7
21 Observing people online (desktop-sharing)	7.0	16	4.8	1	8.3	10	5.7	5
22 Sharing snippets of info online in twitter-like communities	2.2	5	0.0	0	1.7	2	3.4	3

FIGURE 12.1 Learning Activity Preferences by Generation

by generation. Because there was only one traditionalist response, that datum was omitted from the aggregate table. Immediately noticeable is the fact that little variation exists in learning activity preferences according to generation.

The following two important trends jump out when reviewing these results.

Homogeneity across Generations in Learning Activity Preferences

Learning activity preferences across the three generations are strikingly similar in this population. Out of 22 possibilities, "Reviewing information in graphic format (tables, charts, graphs)" was the favorite for millennials, favorite for generation X, and second favorite for baby boomers. "Using search engines for online research" was second favorite for millennials, second favorite for generation X, and third favorite for baby boomers. "Interacting with computer simulations" was fifth favorite for millennials, second favorite for generation X, and favorite for baby boomers. These similarities defy most generational assumptions that digital natives and digital immigrants prefer to use technology differently.

Again, I do not claim to apply these results to all individuals of these generations. Rather I am highlighting the value of studying one's own population before making business decisions based on generalizations. If the manager of Management Development had trusted the gen-experts, he would have been led astray for this particular group because they are more similar than different.

Results were also very similar when analyzing the five least favorite learning activities. All three generations chose "sharing snippets of information online in twitter-like communities" as their least favorite learning activity. "Observing people online (desktop-sharing)" and "participating in multi-user online brainstorming centers" were in each generational cohort's bottom five selections. "Desktop sharing" was second worst for millennials, third worst for generation X, and fifth worst for baby boomers. "Online brainstorming centers" was fifth worst for millennials, second worst for generation X, and fourth worst for baby boomers. Given the group had 22 learning activities from which to choose, it is surprising how consistent these results are.

Even when selecting an activity falling in the middle of the list, the results were consistent. For example, 23.8 percent of baby boomers selected "Presenting your findings to others" as a favorite activity, landing ninth on the list. "Presenting your findings to others" was also ninth on the list for generation X with 24.2 percent, and it was tenth on the list for millennials with 23.9 percent, a difference of less than 0.5 percent across the three generations.

The Lack of Interest in More Advanced, Social-Media Based Technological Solutions from all Generations (but Most Particularly from the Millennials)

The most frequently selected learning activity for all participants regardless of generation was "Reviewing information in graphic format (tables, charts, graphs)." The second most popular selection was "Using search engines for online research." The third most popular selection for all participants was "Interacting with computer simulations." The fourth most popular selection was "Practicing real-world interactions in online simulations." Finally, the fifth most popular selection was "Reviewing quick reference guides such as Frequently Asked Questions (FAQs)."

Interestingly, the above activities are mostly Web 1.0 technologies. Web 1.0 technologies are those technologies that have been available and popular since the inception of the Internet. It is possible the group was primarily selecting learning activities with which they were familiar. Given that all participants worked for the same organization, these may be common learning tools used in the workplace, and, therefore, more familiar.

The least popular selection out of 22 total learning activities was "Sharing snippets of information online in twitter-like communities." The second least popular option was "Observing people online (desktop sharing)," whereas the third least popular option was "Participating in online discussion boards." Two learning activities were tied for fourth least popular. They were "Completing questionnaires and/or a survey" and "Participating in multi-user online brainstorming centers." Finally, the fifth least popular option was "Playing multi-player online games within virtual worlds."

Many of these least popular options are Web 2.0 and Web 3.0 technologies with a focus on social learning and sharing. Web 2.0 is frequently defined as a more collaborative version of the web in which social media and peer-to-peer sharing are the norm whereas Web 3.0 technologies include immersive technologies, such as virtual worlds and multiplayer online role-playing games.

It seems this population did not prefer social learning and peer-to-peer sharing. However, many generational experts argue that millennials have a natural penchant for these kinds of tools. Given the twenty-first-century technological advances and the popularity of social media sites in recreational use, it is not unrealistic to believe these assumptions. However, this is not the case for this particular group. Of all the web 2.0 (or collaborative) activities on the list, the most popular was "Interacting with peers in a social media forum." This appeared fourteenth on the list of 22 among all generations. No social media learning activities appeared in any generation's top 10 list. Therefore, all generational groups expressed the same disinterest in this type of learning. This may be due to the fact that the group is not currently engaged in social media learning in the workplace or, if they are, perhaps the experience has been poor. Regardless, this group defies common knowledge about generational differences.

There are other examples. "Interacting with computer simulations" was most popular among older generations, decreasing in popularity with each generation. It was the number one most popular learning activity among baby boomers with 62 percent. Forty-nine percent of the generation X group selected computer simulations as a preferred learning activity, and only 34 percent of millennials selected this activity as a favorite. Although this was a popular activity for all generations and did appear as a top-five favorite for each cohort, it was interesting to note that a more advanced technology was more popular with older participants. On the other hand, "Designing/drawing concepts visually" became less popular with age. Only 19 percent of baby boomers selected drawing as a favorite activity. Conversely, 27 percent of generation X and 32 percent of millennials selected "drawing" as a preferred activity. This activity could be considered one of the least technological activities on the list and yet was more popular among younger generations—again defying the technogeneration stereotype.

Some trends in the data do reflect the stereotype of the technogeneration. For example, "Playing multiplayer online games within virtual worlds" was more popular among millennials than among generation X and baby boomers. Having said that, it was still only the fifteenth most popular activity out of 22 and is relatively low on the list. Considering the popularity of gaming among millennials, this could be surprising. The video gaming industry earned over $100 billion in revenue in 2014 alone. Given the popularity of these games, the numbers in this study are quite low. It could be that this particular group of individuals is not interested in gaming or perhaps they do not feel gaming is an effective way to facilitate learning.

Similarly, "Using mobile applications to engage in online learning via smart phone devices" was also a relatively unpopular learning activity. For baby boomers, this was the second to last option selected by 5 percent of participants. Only 13 percent of millennials selected this option as a favorite and 15 percent generation X did as well. Although mobile apps are widespread and very popular, they scored low on the list in this survey. The distinction should be made here that although millennials in this group may enjoy using smartphones and mobile apps, they may not feel that this is the best method for learning. This speaks to a larger discussion about the advisability of implementing popular technologies in a learning environment before first analyzing whether or not these technologies are conducive to facilitating learning. It may be that mobile applications are not an effective way to teach adults. Based on the survey results, mobile-application learning would not be preferable for this particular group.

Optimizing the Learning Environment

The third and final question in this study asked how the learning environment can best be optimized to account for a multigenerational workforce.

Instructional Design Optimization Begins with Information

Some researchers argue that training courses should be written in multiple iterations so each learner can participate in tailored training according to their preferred learning style. However, with this particular population at the railroad company, there was little variance in the learning style preferences across the generations. This finding in and of itself is an important tool for training professionals and instructional designers. Rather than focusing on differences, programs can be geared to honor similarities. However, these results are not able to be generalized across all corporate organizations. It is entirely possible that if this survey had been conducted at an Internet start-up or a marketing firm, or even another railroad company, the results would be quite different.

Once the learning-style preferences are collected, training and learning programs can be designed with the preferences of the student population in mind. For example, it might surprise the training and learning leaders at this particular railroad company that observing people online (e.g., desktop sharing) was at the bottom of the list of favorite activities for this participant group among all generations. Although this may be a powerful demonstration tool, this particular group does not prefer it. The suggestion is not to eliminate desktop sharing from all learning, but to heavily weigh or begin class activities with learning tools with which class members are most comfortable. Though this particular group would enjoy classes with online computer simulations, reviewing quick reference guides such as FAQs and using search engines to find information, designers could also include less desirable tools, the inclusion of which research shows are effective. Activities such as game-based learning can be incorporated into training as a secondary or tertiary tool so as not to disengage the player/learners in this group.

Do Not Assume Preferences Based on Generation

According to a 2010 study by the American Society for Training and Development (ASTD), now referred to as the Association of Talent Development (ATD), more than 60 percent of learning professionals said they considered possible generational differences in their approaches to instructional design. Since the generational issue has been at the forefront of corporate learning discussions in recent years, learning professionals are in a position to make curriculum design decisions based on weak, unreliable information that has been widely distributed in corporate circles. As such, instructional designers should be cautious when making assumptions about generational differences.

For example, in this study, millennials did not prefer using web 2.0 technologies in learning. In fact, no generation in this study preferred using social media forums or twitter-like environments in learning, contrary to the popular literature describing it as the cutting-edge in corporate learning. Although this may be the wave of the future, it would be, in fact, somewhat ineffective for this group. Curriculum designers should be wary of creating new programs based on assumptions that millennials like new technologies and baby boomers learn differently from younger generations. This is not to say that these stereotypes are never true. In fact, there might be significant differences across the generations if the organization studied had been a government organization or a high-tech organization. It is entirely possible the millennial employees at Facebook would prefer learning via social media tools. The only way for training and learning leaders to be sure is to survey their learner population internally before designing and developing new training and learning solutions. In fact, the creators of the Index of Learning Styles tool indicated that it was designed to help create effective learning programs. This will require extra time and flexibility on the instructional designer and developer's part, but will help ensure that learning will be optimized to address the learning style preferences of the generationally diverse workforce.

Practical Implications

The results of this engagement with the railroad organization had a number of practical implications for the management development team. First, at the time that this study was taking place, they were in the process of evaluating third-party vendors for a major simulation-based training development effort. The survey results revealed that "Interacting with computer simulations" and "Practicing real-world interactions in online simulations" were the third and fourth favorite learning activities across all generations. In seeing this, the leadership team used this survey to justify the significant investment in the simulation-based training.

More importantly, however, the leadership team was surprised to learn that there were few differences in learning preferences across the three generations of employees in their program. This finding was surprising not only to the manager of the program, but also to his superiors and other team members. In presenting this study to the leadership team, they discussed the errors they had made in assuming generational differences. They also discussed other ways in which generational assumptions were being made in the company. This valuable lesson sparked a shift in how the executive team thinks about generational differences, and hopefully led to greater understanding for the employees.

Resources: Case Study 2 Details

The following appendix provides further detail into the research results presented in Chapter 12: Case Study 2. The purpose of the study was to identify learning-style preferences by generational cohort as well as learning-activity preferences by generational cohort. Three research questions were asked:

1. To what extent do learning-style preferences vary by generational cohort?
2. To what extent do preferences for learning technologies and learning activities vary by generational cohort?
3. How can instructional design for web-based learning be optimized to address the learning-style preferences of a generationally diverse workforce?

The first part of the survey, related to learning style and question one, was a tool called the Index of Learning Styles (ILS) developed by Richard Felder and Barbara Soloman. The ILS is a 44-item web-based survey designed to identify an individual's learning-style preferences. Felder and Soloman designed the instrument in 1991, and based their work on the four dimensions of the Felder-Silverman learning style model (Felder & Silverman, 1988). The ILS measures learning preferences on four dimensions: (1) active (i.e., learning by doing) versus reflective (i.e., learning by thinking), (2) sensing (i.e., practical and fact-based) versus intuitive (i.e., theoretical and abstract), (3) visual (i.e., learning via images) versus verbal (i.e., learning via writing or speech), and (4) sequential (steplike linearity) versus global (holistic).

Results are presented for each dimension along a range of odd integers. Eleven questions are posed for each dimension and there are two possible answers for each question. One answer translates to a value of +1 while the other answer translates to a value of –1.

ACT						X					REF
11	9	7	5	3	1	1	3	5	7	9	11
SEN						X					INT
11	9	7	5	3	1	1	3	5	7	9	11
VIS						X					VRB
11	9	7	5	3	1	1	3	5	7	9	
SEQ						X					GLO
11	9	7	5	3	1	1	3	5	7	9	11

If your score on a scale is 1–3, you are fairly well balanced on the two dimensions of that scale. If your score on a scale is 5–7, you have a moderate preference for one dimension on the scale and will learn more easily in a teaching environment favoring that dimension. If your score on a scale is 9–11, you have a very strong preference for one dimension of the scale. You may have real difficulty learning in an environment that does not support that preference.

A number of academic scholars have conducted studies to assess the reliability, factor structure, and construct validity of the ILS. Four studies in particular studied the reliability of the tool. All found that the tool was valid and reliable on all dimensions. There was one exception, however, in the sequential-global dimension, which did not meet the criterion for attitude surveys in one study. However, on the whole, these studies suggest the ILS is a sufficiently reliable and valid instrument for assessing learning styles.

Felder and Spurlin (2005) clarified that the intended use of this tool was to suggest behavioral tendencies along a continuum but was not a reliable indicator of skill, nor should it be considered a fixed measurement, given learners' preferences can evolve over time.

One metastudy conducted by the tool creators calculated the average responses from 17 studies (2,506 total participants) that used the Felder-Soloman ILS to understand the average learner distribution on the four dimensions. Table R.1 displays the learning-style distribution in this metastudy. Table R.2 displays the learning-style distribution for all respondents in the railroad study. The active dimension was higher than the reflective dimension in both the metastudy (64.0 percent) and in this study (63.0 percent). Sensing was also higher than the intuitive dimension, 63.0 percent in the metastudy and 65.2 percent in this study. The metastudy found the same overwhelming preference for visual learning (82 percent) as in this study (85.7 percent). The greatest variance was found in the sequential versus global dimension. In the metastudy, the sequential dimension was slightly higher (60.0 percent) than that of this study (55.7 percent), although not by much.

TABLE R.1 Summary of Average Learning Style Preferences: 17 previous studies ($N = 2,506$)

	Percent (%)	*n*		Percent (%)	*n*
Active	64.0	1,604	**Reflective**	36.0	902
Sensing	63.0	1,579	**Intuitive**	37.0	927
Visual	82.0	2,055	**Verbal**	18.0	451
Sequential	60.0	1,504	**Global**	40.0	1,002

Source: Felder and Brent (2005).

TABLE R.2 Summary of Average Learning Style Preferences: All Generations ($N = 230$)

	Percent (%)	*n*		Percent (%)	*n*
Active	63.0	145	**Reflective**	37.0	85
Sensing	65.2	150	**Intuitive**	34.8	80
Visual	85.7	197	**Verbal**	14.3	33
Sequential	55.7	128	**Global**	44.3	102

TABLE R.3 Summary of Learning Style Preferences by Generation: Millennials ($N = 89$)

	Percent (%)	*n*		Percent (%)	*n*
Active	60.0	53	**Reflective**	40.0	36
Sensing	70.8	63	**Intuitive**	29.2	26
Visual	84.3	75	**Verbal**	15.7	14
Sequential	58.4	52	**Global**	41.6	37

Table R.3 displays the results for millennials at the railroad. For millennials in this study, 60 percent of respondents were classified as active learners as compared to 64 percent overall in the metastudy mentioned earlier. Seventy-one percent were sensing learners in this study as compared to 63 percent in the metastudy. Eighty-four percent of the millennials were classified as visual learners, only slightly higher than the metastudy results (82 percent). Finally, 58 percent of millennials preferred the sequential dimension compared to the average of 60 percent in the metastudy.

The research results for generation X revealed similar results. Table R.4 presents a summary of data for learning style preferences of generation X. The active dimension was preferred at a rate of 67 percent, compared with 64 percent in the metastudy. The sensing dimension was preferred at a rate of 61 percent, compared to 63 percent. The visual dimension was overwhelmingly preferred at 87 percent, compared to

TABLE R.4 Summary of Learning Style Preferences by Generation: Generation X (N = 119)

	Percent (%)	n		Percent (%)	n
Active	67.2	80	**Reflective**	32.8	39
Sensing	61.3	73	**Intuitive**	38.7	46
Visual	87.4	104	**Verbal**	12.6	15
Sequential	58.0	69	**Global**	42.0	50

82 percent in the metastudy. Finally, the sequential dimension was preferred at 59 percent compared to 60 percent.

Finally, Table R.5 presents a summary of data for learning-style preferences of the baby boomers. The active dimension was preferred by 57 percent of baby boomers compared to a 64 percent in the metastudy. The sensing dimension was preferred by baby boomers at a rate of 67 percent; the average in the metastudy was 63 percent. The visual dimension was preferred by baby boomers at a rate of 81 percent as compared to an average of 82 percent in the metastudy. However, the sequential dimension is where some variance is found. In this study, 33 percent of baby boomers preferred the sequential dimension. In the metastudy, the sequential dimension was preferred by 60 percent of participants. The research seems to indicate that although most individuals prefer learning using a step-by-step approach, the baby boomers in this group prefer

TABLE R.5 Summary of Learning Style Preferences by Generation: Baby Boomers (N = 21)

	Percent (%)	n		Percent (%)	n
Active	57.1	12	**Reflective**	42.9	9
Sensing	66.7	14	**Intuitive**	33.3	7
Visual	81.0	17	**Verbal**	19.0	4
Sequential	33.3	7	**Global**	66.7	14

learning in a holistic manner. It is important to note, however, the small sample size of the baby boomer cohort in this study.

Due to the low response rate of the traditionalist generation ($n = 1$), generational results were only calculated for the baby boomers, generation X, and millennials.

References

Angell, Roger. 1953. "Youth and the World: U.S.A." *Holiday*, March, 55–59.

ASTD Research. 2010. *Instructional Systems Design: Today and in the Future*. Research Report. Alexandria, VA: ASTD Press.

Bach, Richard. 1989. *Illusions: The Adventures of a Reluctant Messiah*. New York: Dell.

Bach, Richard. 2014. *Jonathan Livingston Seagull: The Complete Edition*. New York: Scribner.

Bolton, Robyn. "Whole Foods' Misguided Play for Millennials." *Harvard Business Review*, May 14, 2015 There is no volume number: https://hbr .org/2015/05/whole-foods-misguided-play-for-millennials.

Bureau of Labor Statistics. 2014. "America's Young Adults at 27: Labor Market Activity, Education and Household Composition: Results from a Longitudinal Survey." News release, Washington, DC: U.S. Department of Labor.

Bureau of Labor Statistics. 2015. "Volunteering in the United States, 2014." News Release, Washington, DC: Bureau of Labor Statistics.

Cisco. 2015. *Cisco Blogs*. San Jose: Cisco. http://blogs.cisco.com/tag/ millennials

Copeland, Craig. 2010 "Employee Tenure Trend Lines, 1983–2010." Monthly newsletter, Washington DC: Employee Benefit Research Institute.

The Coshocton Tribune. 1920. "London Baby Boom." August 7, 4.

Coupland, Douglas. 1991. *Generation X: Tales for an Accelerated Culture*. New York: St. Martin's Griffin.

The Council of Economic Advisers. 2014. *15 Economic Facts About Millennials*. Washington, DC: Executive Office of the President of the United States.

Crowne, Douglas P., and David Marlowe. 1960. "A New Scale of Social Desirability Independent of Psychopathology." *Journal of Consulting Psychology*: 349–354. *24*(4)

Doran, George T. 1981. "There's an S.M.A.R.T. Way to Write Management's Goals and Objectives." *Management Review*, November: 35–36. *70.11*

Elance-O-Desk. 2015. *Millennials and the Workplace in 2015*. Mountain View, CA: Elance-O-Desk.

Espinoza, Chip, Mick Ukleja, and Craig Rusch. 2010. *Managing the Millennials: Discover the Core Competencies for Managing Today's Workforce*. Hoboken, NJ: John Wiley & Sons.

Fallon, Nicole. 2014. "Modern Women Favor Marketing That Defies Stereotypes." *Business News Daily*, September 30.

Felder, R. M., & J., Spurlin (2005). Applications, reliability and validity of the index of learning styles. *International Journal of Engineering Education*, *21*(1), 103-112.

Felder, R. M., & L. K., Silverman (1988). Learning and teaching styles in engineering education. *Journal of Engineering Education*, *78*(7), 674-681. Retrieved from http://www.ncsu.edu/felder-public/Papers/LS-1988.pdf

Felder, Richard M., and Barbara A. Soloman. 2004. *Index of Learning Styles Questionnaire*. Raleigh: North Carolina State University. https://www.engr.ncsu.edu/learningstyles/ilsweb.html

Frumkin, Tamar. 2015. *5 Ways Millennials are Re-defining the Customer Experience*. Blog. San Francisco: Salesforce. https://www.salesforce.com/blog/2015/04/5-ways-millennials-re-defining-customer-experience-gp.html

Futurecast. 2015. *Money Matters: How Affluent Millennials Are Living the Millennial Dream*. Kansas City: Futurecast.

The Galveston Daily News. 1941. "Baby Boom Increases Population of U.S." December.

Gladwell, Malcolm. 2000. *The Tipping Point: How Little Things Can Make a Big Difference*. Boston: Little, Brown and Company.

Hamblett, Charles, and Jane Deverson. 1964. *Generation X*. London: Tandem.

Hersey, Paul, Kenneth H. Blanchard, and Dewey E. Johnson. 2012. *Management of Organizational Behavior: Leading Human Resources*. 10th ed. Upper Saddle River, NJ: Prentice Hall.

Hole, David, Le Zhong, and Jeff Schwartz. 2010. *Talking About Whose Generation?* Deloitte Review, New York: Deloitte Development LLC.

Holyoke, Laura, and Erick Larson. 2009. "Engaging the Adult Learner Generational Mix." *Journal of Adult Education*: 12–21. *38*(1)

Howe, Neil, and William Strauss. 1991. *Generations: The History of America's Future, 1584 to 2089*. New York: William Morrow and Company, Inc.

2000. *Millennials Rising: The Next Great Generation*. New York: Vintage.

IBM Institute for Business Value. 2014. *Myths, Exaggerations and Uncomfortable Truths: The Real Story Behind Millennials in the Workplace*. Somers, NY: IBM.

Johnson, Meagan, and Larry, Johnson. 2010. *Generations Inc.: From Boomers to Linksters- Managing the Friction Between Generations at Work*. New York: AMA.

Jones, Landon Y. 2008. *Great Expectations: America & the Baby Boom Generation*. New York: Coward, McCann & Geoghegan.

Kelton. 2013. *The State of Workplace Productivity Report*. Report, Santa Monica, CA: Cornerstone OnDemand.

Lahey, Joanna N. 2005. "Do Older Workers Face Discrimination?" *Center for Retirement Research*: 1–8.

Lancaster, Lynne C. 2004. "When Generations Collide: How to Solve the Generational Puzzle at Work." *The Management Forum Series*. New York: HarperCollins Publishers Inc.

Lester, Scott W., Rhetta L. Standifer, Nicole J. Schultz, and James M. Windsor. 2012. "Actual Versus Perceived Generational Differences at Work: An Empirical Examination." *Journal of Leadership & Organizational Studies:* 340–354. *19*(3)

Lewis, Gary J., and Timothy C. Bates. 2010. "Genetic Evidence for Multiple Biological Mechanisms Underlying In-Group Favoritism." *Psychological Science*: 1623–1628. *21*(11)

Maslow, Abraham H. 1954. *Motivation and Personality*. New York: Harper & Row.

McCrindle, Mark. 2013. *The 5 Global Generations Defined by Name, Year of Birth, and Social Influences*. Bella Vista: McCrindle Research. http://www.slideshare.net/markmccrindle/generations-definedsociologically

Mehra, Chetna. 2015. "Millennials Want to Do Something That Is Meaningful, Says Author Jamie Notter." *BusinessLine on Campus*, August 5.

Monthly Labor Review. 2013. *Civilian Labor Force Participation Rates by Age, Sex, Race, and Ethnicity*. Washington, DC: Bureau of Labor Statistics, 2013.

Neck, Chris C., and Charles P. Manz. 2012. *Mastering Self Leadership: Empowering Yourself for Personal Excellence* (6th ed.). Upper Saddle River, NJ: Prentice Hall.

Nielsen. 2014. *Millennials: Technology = Social Connection*. New York: Nielsen.

O'Donnell, J.T. 2015. 6 Things Millennials Say at Work (and What They Really Mean). Blog. Inc. http://www.inc.com/jt-odonnell/6-things-millennials-say-at-work-and-what-they-really-mean.html

Oxford Economics and SAP. *Workforce 2020. Social Media Research Hub*. Newton Square, PA: SAP, 2015.

Pew Research Center. 2010a. *Baby Boomers Retire*. Washington, DC: Pew Research Center.

Pew Research Center. 2010b. *Millennials: A Portrait of Generation Next: Confident. Connected. Open to Change*. Research Report, Washington, DC: Pew Research Center.

Pew Research Center. 2011. *Angry Silents, Disengaged Millennials: The Generation Gap and the 2012 Election*. Research Report, Washington, DC: Pew Research Center.

Pew Research Center. 2014. *Millennials in Adulthood: Detached from Institutions, Networked with Friends*. Research Report, Washington DC: Pew Research Center.

Prensky, Mark. 2001. "Digital Natives, Digital Immigrants." *On the Horizon:* 1–6. *9*(5)

PricewaterhouseCoopers; University of Southern California; London Business School. 2013. *PwC's NextGen: A Global Generational Study*. Research Report, New York: PwC.

Rock, David. 2009. *Your Brain at Work: Strategies for Overcoming Distraction, Regaining Focus, and Working Smarter All Day Long*. New York: HarperCollins.

Salveo Partners, LLC. n.d. "How to Become a Place Where Millennials Want to Work." Blog. http://salveopartners.com/how-to-become-a-place-where-millennials-want-to-work/

Salzberg, Barry. 2012. "What Millennials Want Most: A Career That Actually Matters." *Forbes Leadership*, July 3. http://www.forbes.com/sites/forbesleadershipforum/2012/07/03/what-millennials-want-most-a-career-that-actually-matters/

Schullery, Nancy M. 2013. "Workplace Engagement and Generational Differences in Values." *Business Communication Quarterly*, March 4: 252–265.

Selwyn, Neil. 2009. "The Digital Native—Myth and Reality." *Aslib Proceedings: New Information Perspectives* (2009): 364–379. *61*(4)

Senge, Peter M. 2006. *The Fifth Discipline: The Art & Practice of The Learning Organization*. New York: Random House Audio.

Smith, Jacquelyn. 2014. "Why Millennials Need Constant Feedback At Work." *Business Insider*.

Sujansky, Joanne, and Jan Ferri-Reed. 2009. *Keeping The Millennials: Why Companies Are Losing Billions in Turnover to this Generation—and What to Do About It*. Hoboken, NJ: John Wiley & Sons.

Tajfel, Henry, and John Turner. 1979. "An Integrative Theory of Intergroup Conflict." In *The Social Psychology of Intergroup Relations*, edited by Henry Tajfel, 33–47.

Thomas, Susan G. 2011. "The Divorce Generation." *Wall Street Journal*, July 9.

Tuckman, Bruce W. 1965. "Developmental Sequence in Small Groups." *Psychological Bulletin:* 384–399. *63*(6)

Tulgan, Bruce. 2009. *Not Everyone Gets a Trophy: How to Manage Generation Y.* San Francisco: Jossey-Bass.

Twenge, Jean M., and Stacy M. Campbell. 2008. "Generational Differences in Psychological Traits and Their Impact on the Workplace." *Journal of Managerial Psychology*: 862–877. *23*(8)

Ulrich, John McAllister, and Andrea L. Harris. 2003. *GenXegesis*. Madison: University of Wisconsin Press, 2003.

Universum; INSEAD Emering Markets Institute; The HEAD Foundation. 2014a. *Our Evolution…How Experience Changes Millennials: We Look In-Depth at How Age and Gender Influence Millennial Attitudes to Work.* Research Report, Universum.

Universum; INSEAD Emering Markets Institute; The HEAD Foundation. 2014b. *Our Greatest Fears: Examining Millennials' Concerns About Career, Retirement, and Quality of Life—and the Steps You Should Take to Address Them.* Research Report, Universum.

Universum; INSEAD Emering Markets Institute; The HEAD Foundation. 2014c. *Support Me But Don't Tell Me What To Do: Who and What Influences Millennials' Career Choices? The Answers Aren't As Clear-Cut As One Might Think*. Research Report, Universum.

Universum; INSEAD Emering Markets Institute; The HEAD Foundation. 2014d. *Understanding a Misunderstood Generation: The First Large-Scale Study of How Millennial Attitudes and Actions Vary Across the Globe, and the Implications for Employers*. Research Report, Universum.

Universum; INSEAD Emering Markets Institute; The HEAD Foundation. 2014e. *We Are More Different Than You Think: A Look at the Diversity of Millennial Ideas and Attitudes Within Regions, and the Implications for Employers*. Research Report, Universum.

Universum; INSEAD Emering Markets Institute; The HEAD Foundation. 2014f. *You Got Us Wrong: Millennials Prove They Are Diverse in Their Career Aspirations and Desire for Work-Life Balance*. Research Report, Universum.

Walker, J. D., and Linda Jorn. 2009. *21st Century Students: Technology Survey*. University Report, Twin Cities: University of Minnesota Twin Cities Office of Information Technology.

About the Author

D r. Jessica Kriegel works as an organizational development consultant for Oracle Corporation, where she acts as an adviser and strategist in matters of organizational development, change management, and talent development.

In 2013, Jessica completed her doctoral degree in educational leadership and management with a specialization in human resources development from Drexel University. Her doctoral dissertation research focused on intergenerational dynamics. After graduating she became an adjunct faculty member for the Masters in Human Resources Development program.

As a result of her work in the field, Oracle has named Jessica an Oracle Thought Leader. She is regular contributor to *Forbes* and speaks at conferences throughout the year on intergenerational issues.

Jessica also has an MBA in International Business from Hult International Business School, completed in 2008.

She sits on the board of the Downtown Sacramento Partnership, the Sacramento Philharmonic & Opera Street Soccer USA - Sacramento Chapter, and the Nehemiah Emerging Leaders Alumni Association.

She was awarded the Association of Talent Development's "One to Watch" Award in 2015, and *Training* magazine's "Emerging Training Leaders Award" One to Watch in 2014. She was *Sacramento Business Journal*'s 40 Under 40 in 2015, and valedictorian of her Drexel University graduating class in 2013.

Index

Note: Page references in *italics* refer to figures.

A

Above-average effect, 70
Affluence, marketing and, 41
Age discrimination, 15–24
  age and generation, definitions, 17
  Age Discrimination in Employment Act
    (ADEA), 18–19
  defined, 17–19
  depression and anxiety issues, 24
  hiding, behind generation labels, 21–22
  overview, 19–21
  social approval and, 23
Ambition
  performance management and, 81
  stereotypes about, 51, 54
Angell, Roger, 5
Anxiety, age discrimination and, 24
Assessment
  for collaborative teamwork, 103
  of organizational culture, 143–144
  return on investment (ROI) for training,
    Oracle (case study), 185–191
  survey for needs assessment (Oracle case
    study), 152–166
  survey for needs assessment (railroad
    organization case study), 198–200,
    211–216, *213, 214, 215*
  See also Performance review
Association of Talent Development (ATD),
  208

B

Baby Boomers
  age discrimination and, 20
  defined, xviii–xix
  term creation, 5

Bates, Timothy, 13
Beliefs, stereotypes as, 7–9
Bias, awareness of, 68–69
Blanchard, Kenneth H., 87
Boston College, 17
Brain, categorization by, 6–7
Branding, by employers, 114–115, 118, 174
Bureau of Labor Statistics, xxv, 114

C

Campbell, Stacey, 22–24
Capa, Robert, 5
Categorization, 6–7, 11–14
Catz, Safra, 148
Center for Retirement Research (Boston
  College), 17
Change agents, 140
China, generational stereotypes in, 27–29
Cisco, 99
Civil Rights Act of 1964, 18
Collaborative teamwork, 95–108
  importance of, 103
  stereotypes, overcoming, 102–107
  stereotypes about, 97–98, 99–102
  technology and, 130
Communication
  communication materials for organizational
    change, 141–142
  between managers and Millennials (Oracle
    case study), 182, 183–184
Compensation, employee engagement and,
  60–62
Conversations, about stereotypes, 139, 142
Cornerstone OnDemand, 100, 125, 126
Coupland, Douglas, 5

Culture. *See* Globalization; Organizational culture change
Customer relationship management (CRM), 42–43

D

Decision making, for collaborative teamwork, 103–104
Depression, age discrimination and, 24
Development, professional, 81
Deverson, Jane, 5
Digital Native, The (Selwyn), 54
Digital Natives, Digital Immigrants (Prensky), 128
"Digital natives"/"digital immigrants," defined, 116, 128
Diversity
  collaborative teamwork and, 100–101
  of Millennials, 54–55, 58–59
  for organizational culture change, 140–141
Divorce, 20, 51
Doran, George, 88

E

Efficiency, 77–78
Elance-o-Desk, 102
Ellison, Larry, 147
Emotional intelligence, 151
Employee Benefits Research Institute, 113
Employee engagement, 47–71
  collaborative work environment and, 100
  Millennials, motivating, 60–62
  Millennials, stereotypes, 47–60
  overcoming stereotypes for, 63–71
Employer brand
  Oracle case study on, 174
  for recruitment, 114–115, 118
Encouragement, need for, 79–80
Entitlement, stereotypes about, 59, 81
Equal Employment Opportunity Commission, 17
Espinoza, Chip, xxiv
Esteem needs, 66–67

F

Face-to-face contact, technology preferences compared to, 127–128
Feedback

performance management and, 78–79, 80, 89, 90
  for training (Oracle case study), 187–188
  See also Performance review
Felder, Richard, 197, 198, 200–207, 211–216
Ferri-Reed, Jan, xxiv, 177
Fifth Discipline, The (Senge), 9
"5 Ways Millennials are Re-defining the Customer Experience" (Frumkin), 42–43
Focus groups, 166–168
Forming stage, for teams, 106
Frumkin, Tamar, 42–43
Futurecast, 41

G

Games, for training, 176
Gender, marketing and, 40–41
"Generational Differences in Psychological Traits and Their Impact on the Workplace" (Twenge, Campbell), 22–24
Generational issues, xvii–xxvi
  exercise, xviii–xix
  generation, defined, 17
  intergenerational conflict (Oracle case study) on, 161–165, 171
  overview, xvii–xviii
  perception and, xix–xxii
  problem of labeling, xxii–xxvi
  See also Collaborative teamwork; Employee engagement; Labeling; Oracle (case study); Organizational culture change; Performance management; Railroad organization (case study); Recruiting; Technology
Generations (Howe, Strauss), 6
Generations Inc. (Johnson, Johnson), xxv, 177
Generation X
  defined, xviii–xix
  Millennial stereotypes related to, 51
  term creation, 5–6
Generation X (Hamblett, Deverson), 5
Generation X: Tales for an Accelerated Culture (Coupland), 5
Generation Y. *See* Millennials
Gen-experts, defined, xxiii
Gladwell, Malcolm, 137
Globalization, 25–33

collaborative teamwork and, 101
generational stereotypes in non-U.S.
    cultures, 25–31
online communication preferences and, 116
overcoming Western dominance in global
    environment, 31–32
performance review and, 84
U.S. workforce statistics, 25
work/life balance perception and, 69
Goals
    creating development goals for employees,
        91
    personal goals of employees, 88–89
    setting, for collaborative strategy, 105
Goleman, Daniel, 151

H

Hamblett, Charles, 5
HEAD, 69, 101, 115, 127
"Helicopter parenting," 53
Hersey, Paul, 87
Hierarchy of Needs (Maslow), 63–68
Hole, David, 27
Holiday, 5
Holyoke, Laura, 85
Howe, Neil, xxiv, 6
Human resources (HR)
    compensation and employee engagement,
        60–62
    generational issues as concern to, xvii
    recruiting and age discrimination, 17
    See also Oracle (case study); Performance
        management; Railroad organization
        (case study); Recruiting
Hurd, Mark, 148

I

IBM. *See* Institute for Business Values'
    Millennial Survey 2014 (IBM)
Icebreaker games, for training, 176
Illusory superiority, 70
Index of Learning Styles (ILS) (Felder,
    Soloman), 197, 198, 200–207, *202*,
    211–216, *213, 214, 215*
India, generational stereotypes in, 30
Inference, 9–11
In-group/out-group dynamics, 11–14

INSEAD Emerging Market Institute, 69, 101,
    115, 127
Instant gratification, 59–60
Institute for Business Values' Millennial
    Survey 2014 (IBM)
    collaborative teamwork and, 99–101, 105
    employee engagement and, 58, 70
    performance management issues and, 83,
        84, 86, 88
    recruiting and, 115, 116
    technology and, 124, 127
Interstate Commerce Commission (ICC), 195

J

Japan, generational stereotypes in, 29
Job satisfaction, Oracle case study on,
    165–166
Johnson, Dewey E., 87
Johnson, Larry, xxv, 177
Johnson, Meagan, xxv, 177
Journal of Adult Education, 85
*Journal of Leadership and Organizational
    Studies*, 124–125
Journal of Management, 61
Journal of Managerial Psychology, 22–24

K

Keeping the Millennials (Sujansky, Ferri-Reed),
    xxiv, 177
Kurian, Thomas, 148

L

Labeling
    age discrimination and, 15–24
    divisiveness of, 92–93
    globalization and, 25–33
    problem of, xxii–xxvi
    stereotyping and, 3–14 (*See also*
        Stereotypes)
    usefulness of, 35–43
    See also Stereotypes
Ladder of Inference, 9–11
Lahey, Joanna, 17
Lancaster, Lynne, xxiii
Larson, Erick, 85
Laziness, stereotypes about, 56
Lester, Scott W., 13, 83
Lewis, Gary, 13

London Business School, 31
Love/belonging needs, 65–66
Loyalty, of employees, 111–112, 113–114

M
"Making Stuff Up (MSU)," 8–9
Manager-employee relationship. *See*
 Performance management
Managing the Millennials (Espinoza, Ukleja,
 Rusch), xxiii
Manz, Charles, 180–181
Marketing, labeling usefulness for, 35–43
Maslow, Abraham, 63–68
Mastering Self Leadership (Neck, Manz),
 180–181
Mavens, 137
McCrindle, Mark, 32
Meaning, of work, 53
Millennial Branding, 102
Millennial Majority Workforce
 (Elance-o-Desk, Millennial Branding),
 102
Millennials
 age discrimination and, 21–22
 defined, xviii–xix
 marketing to, 38–40
 term creation, 6
 work/life balance values of, 32 (*See also*
  Work/life balance)
 See also Collaborative teamwork; Employee
  engagement; Globalization; Labeling;
  Oracle (case study); Organizational
  culture change; Performance
  management; Railroad organization
  (case study); Recruiting; Stereotypes;
  Technology
Millennials Rising (Howe, Strauss), xxiv
Motivation. *See* Employee engagement
Motivation and Personality (Maslow), 63–68

N
Narcissism, 80
Neck, Chris, 180–181
Needs assessment
 Index of Learning Styles (ILS) (Felder,
  Soloman), 197, 198, 200–207, *202*,
  211–216, *213*, *214*, *215*
 Oracle survey for (case study), 152–158

Oracle survey results (case study), 159–166
 railroad organization (case study), 198–200
Neuroleadership, 6–7
Nielsen Company, 20
Norming stage, for teams, 106–107

O
O'Donnell, J. T., 52–53
Oracle (case study), 145–192
 background, 147–149
 focus groups, 166–168
 hiring issues, 150–151
 needs assessment survey, 152–158
 needs assessment survey, results, 159–166
 Oracle College Hire (OCH) program,
  148–149, 152–153
 organization development consulting
  (ODC) team, 149
 return on investment (ROI) analysis,
  185–191
 training program for managers, 168–175
 training program for new hires, 168–170,
  175–185
Organizational culture change, 135–144
 acclimating to (Oracle case study), 160–161
 campaign for, 142–143
 change agents of, 140
 collaborative teamwork and, 104–105
 collateral review for, 141–142
 diversity for, 140–141
 evaluation of, 143–144
 mavens of, 137
 questioning stereotypes for, 138–139
 role modeling for, 138
Oxford Economics (SAP), 85

P
Perception
 as reality, xix–xxii
 stereotypes and, 9–11
Performance management, 73–94
 development, 76, 85–86, 91–93
 Oracle program for managers (case study),
  168–175 (*See also* Oracle (case study))
 overcoming stereotypes for, 86–93
 performance review, 76, 84–85, 89–91
 planning and, 75, 82–84, 88–89
 stereotypes about, 75–82

Performance review
performance management and, 76, 84–85, 89–91
360-degree evaluation, 70–71
Performing stage, for teams, 107
Pew Research Center
collaborative teamwork, 100–102
employee engagement, 54
performance management, 83
recruiting, 111
technology, 124, 125, 126, 128, 129
Physiological needs, 64
Prensky, Marc, 128
PricewaterhouseCoopers, 31
Professional development, 81
Profiling. *See* Stereotypes

R
Railroad organization (case study), 193–216
background, 195–198
learning style/activity differences by generation, 199–207, *202*, 211–216, *213*, *214*, *215*
management implications, 209–210
needs assessment, 198–200
optimizing learning environment, 207–209
Recruiting, 95–108
Oracle hiring issues (case study), 150–151
Oracle training program for new hires (case study), 168–170, 175–185
railroad organization hiring issues (case study), 196–198
stereotypes, overcoming, 116–119
stereotypes affecting, 112–116
talent gap and, 111–112
Reich, Robert, 111
Relationships, building, 181
Retention
Oracle case study on, 190–191
stereotypes about, 111–112, 113–114
Rock, David, 6–7
Role models, 138
Rusch, Craig, xxiii
Russia, generational stereotypes in, 30–31

S
Safety needs, 65
Sandberg, Sheryl, 40

SAP, 85
Schultz, Nicole J., 13, 83
Schwartz, Jeff, 27
Self-actualization, 67–68
Self-management, 180–181
Selwyn, Neil, 54, 128
Senge, Peter, 9
Silent Generation
age discrimination and, 19
defined, xviii–xix
term creation, 5
Situational leadership, 87
SMART (specific, measurable, attainable, relevant, timely) objectives, 88
Social approval, need for, 23
Social categorization, 12
Social comparison, 12–13
Social identification, 12
Social media. *See* Technology
Soloman, Barbara, 197, 198, 211–216
South Africa, generational stereotypes in, 29
South Korea, generational stereotypes in, 29–30
Standifer, Rhetta L., 13, 83
State of Workplace Productivity Report, The (Cornerstone OnDemand), 100, 125, 126
Stereotypes, 3–14
age discrimination, 15–24
as beliefs, 7–9
brain and categorization, 6–7
early studies of, 5–6
in-group/out-group dynamics and, 11–14
in non-U.S. cultures, 25–31 (*See also* Globalization)
perception and, xix–xxii, 9–11
questioning, 138–139
See also Labeling; Organizational culture change
Storming stage, for teams, 106
Strauss, William, xxiv, 6
Sujansky, Joanne, xxiv, 177
Surveys
needs assessment (Oracle case study), 152–166
needs assessment (railroad organization case study), 198–207, *202*, 211–216, *213*, *214*, *215*

T

Tajfel, Henri, 11–14
Talent gap, 111–112
"Talking About Whose Generation?" (Hole, Zhong, Schwartz), 27
Technology, 121–131
  employee engagement of Millennials and, 53–54, 55, 57
  marketing and, 38–40, 42–43
  online communication preferences, 116
  online learning (Oracle case study), 172–173
  performance management and, 77, 78, 79, 81, 82, 86
  social media and, xxi
  stereotypes, overcoming, 128–131
  stereotypes about, 123–128
  See also Railroad organization (case study)
Thomas, Susan, 20
360-degree evaluation, 70–71
Title VII, Civil Rights Act of 1964, 18
Toolkit for managers. *See* Collaborative teamwork; Employee engagement; Performance management; Recruiting; Technology
Training
  learning style/activity differences by generation (railroad organization case study), 199–207, *202*, 211–216, *213*, *214*, *215*
  Oracle program for managers (case study), 168–175
  Oracle program for new hires (case study), 168–170, 175–185
  for organizational culture change, 142–143
Tuckman, Bruce, 105–106

Turner, John, 11–14
Turnover, of employees, 111–112, 113–114
Twenge, Jean, 22–24

U

Ukleja, Mick, xxiii
University of California at Berkeley, 111
University of Central Florida, 86
University of Edinburgh, 13
University of London, 54
University of Minnesota, 86
University of Southern California, 31
University of Wisconsin, 13
Universum, 31, 32, 69, 101, 119
"Us," *versus* "them," 11–12

W

Wall Street Journal, 20
Whole Foods, 41–42
Wikipedia, 39
Windsor, James M., 13, 83
Work ethic, stereotypes about, 76–77
Workforce 2020, 85
Work/life balance
  employee engagement and, 55–56, 57–58, 63–69
  globalization and, 32
  Oracle case study on, 174, 179

Y

"Youth and the World" (Angell), 5

Z

Zhong, Le, 27